FOUR CORNERS USA

WONDERS OF THE AMERICAN SOUTHWEST

JIM TURNER

PHOTOGRAPHY BY
LARRY LINDAHL

RIO NUEVO
PUBLISHERS

Rio Nuevo Publishers®
P. O. Box 5250, Tucson, AZ 85703-0250
(520) 623-9558, www.rionuevo.com

Pages ii-iii: Panorama Point vista, Capitol Reef National Park, Utah

Managing Editor: Aaron Downey
Copy Editor: Caroline Cook
Editorial Consultant: John B. Heider
Book design: David Jenney Design
Map: Patti Isaacs, 45th Parallel Maps and Infographics
Shaded relief map base map © Michael Schmeling, aridocean.com

Printed in Korea.

13 12 11 10 9 8 7 6 5 4 3 2

Library of Congress Cataloging-in-Publication Data

Names: Turner, Jim (James Edward), 1949- author.
Title: Four Corners USA / by Jim Turner, with photography by Larry
Lindahl.
Other titles: Four Corners United States of America
Description: Tucson, Arizona : Rio Nuevo Publishers, [2018]
Identifiers: LCCN 2018014532| ISBN 9781940322223 (paperback) |
ISBN
  1940322227 (paperback)
Subjects: LCSH: Four Corners Region—Guidebooks. | Four Corners
  Region—History.
Classification: LCC F788.5 .T87 2018 | DDC 979.2/59—dc23
LC record available at https://lccn.loc.gov/2018014532

+ CONTENTS

Four Corners is an intersection of straight lines,
and while this book is divided into four quadrants,
it also follows a spiral expanding clockwise through
each of the four states. It ends 360 degrees later
almost where it began.

Four Corners USA

- ■ Points of interest
- ▲ Mountain peaks
- ▲ Sacred mountains
- Indian reservations
- National forests
- National parks
- National wilderness areas
- National monuments
- National recreation areas
- Tribal parks
- Freeways
- Secondary highways
- Unimproved roads
- Trail of the Ancients Scenic Byway

UTAH

Manti
Gunnison
Centerfield
Castle Dale
Ferron
Green River
Fillmore
Salina
Richfield
Elsinore
Monroe
FISHLAKE NATIONAL FOREST
DEAD HORSE POINT STATE PARK
CANYONLANDS N. P.
Beaver
Bicknell
Hanksville
CAPITOL
REEF
CANYONLANDS NATIONAL PARK
Escalante
FISHLAKE NATIONAL FOREST
NATIONAL
Newspaper
BEAR
DIXIE NATIONAL
Parowan
Bryce Canyon City
Tropic
GRAND STAIRCASE
GLEN CANYON NATIONAL RECREATION AREA
Bullfrog
BEAR EARS NAT. MON.
NATURAL BRIDGES NATIONAL MON.
MANTI-SAL NATIONAL FORES
Cedar City
CEDAR BREAKS NATIONAL MONUMENT
BRYCE CANYON NATIONAL PARK
NATIONAL MONUMENT
Ferry
Bullfrog Marina
NATIONAL
Enterprise
DIXIE
FOREST
GRAND STAIRCASE-ESCALANTE NATIONAL MONUMENT
EDG THE CE STATE
MONUMENT
ZION NATIONAL PARK
GLEN CANYON DAM
RAINBOW BRIDGE NATIONAL MON.
Navajo Mountain
Goulding's Lodge
GOOSENECKS STATE PARK
Valley of the Gods
Blu
Santa Clara
Saint George
CORAL PINK SAND DUNES STATE PARK
Kanab
The Wave
Navajo Mtn.
Mexican Hat
Colorado City
Fredonia
White Pocket
Paria Canyon
ANTELOPE POINT MARINA
Page
Visitor Center
MONUMENT VALLEY NAVAJO TRIBAL PARK
KAIBAB-PAIUTE INDIAN RES.
VERMILION CLIFFS NATIONAL MONUMENT
HORSESHOE BEND OVERLOOK
KEET SEEL
Agathla Peak (El Capitan)
PIPE SPRING NATIONAL MONUMENT
Lees Ferry
Marble Canyon
NAVAJO INDIAN RESERVATION
BETATIKIN RUIN
NAVAJO NATIONAL MONUMENT
Kayenta
Rock Point
Round
PARIA CANYON-VERMILION CLIFFS WILDERNESS AREA
Shonto
KAIBAB NATIONAL FOREST
Kaibito
Black Mesa
NAVAJO INDIAN RESERVATION
Many Farms
GRAND CANYON-PARASHANT NATIONAL MONUMENT
GRAND
Bitter Springs
Tonalea
HOPI INDIAN RESERVATION
LAKE MEAD NATIONAL REC. AREA
CANYON
Tuba City
DINOSAUR TRACKS
Pinon
Chin
GRAND CANYON NATIONAL PARK
Grand Canyon Village
NATIONAL
Moenkopi
HOPI CULTURAL CENTER MUSEUM
Cameron
Old Oraibi
Polacca
HUALAPAI INDIAN RESERVATION
PARK
LITTLE COLORADO RIVER NAVAJO TRIBAL PARK
Shungopavi
Second Mesa
Keams Canyon
Ganad
HUBBE TRADING POS NATIONA HISTORIC SIT
ARIZONA
Valle
White Cone
Peach Springs
WUPATKI NAT'L. MON.
NAVAJO INDIAN RESERVATION
COCONINO NATIONAL FOREST
Grand Falls
Dilkon
San Francisco Peaks
SUNSET CRATER VOLCANO NAT'L. MON.
Humphreys Peak
Leupp
Williams
KAIBAB NATIONAL FOREST
Flagstaff
PAINTED DESERT COUNTY PARK
CIBOLA
Kachina Village
WALNUT CANYON NAT'L. MON.
HOMOLOVI STATE PARK
Oak Creek Canyon
Meteor Crater
Winslow
Joseph City
Holbrook
PETR FOR NATI
Paulden
Sedona
COCONINO NATIONAL FOREST
Painted Desert

0   50 Miles
0   50 Kilometers

> *"Elsewhere the sky is the roof of the world; but here the earth was the floor of the sky."*
>
> —WILLA CATHER,
> *Death Comes for the Archbishop*, 1927

The slot canyons near Page, Arizona, are a phenomenal example of nature's wondrous sandstone sculptures.

OPPOSITE: Monument Valley is the heart and spirit of the Colorado Plateau's far-reaching landscapes and barren beauty.

IN THE MIDDLE OF NOWHERE ON the red sandstone Colorado Plateau, two straight lines cross at right angles and form a "quadripoint." Coined by the Office of the Geographer of the United States in 1964, a quadripoint exists when the borders of four distinct territories come together. There is only one place in the United States where four states intersect: Arizona, Utah, Colorado, and New Mexico. For more than a century and a half, the area of roughly 150 miles in each direction has been known as "Four Corners," most of which lies on a geographical feature known as the Colorado Plateau. To Southwesterners, "Four Corners," means not only the vast expanse of magnificent rock formations, vistas, and skies, but also a wide variety of people who live there, along with their histories, customs, and cultures.

Some people see the area as forbidding and desolate at first, but once they get used to the differences, many learn to appreciate the panoramic landscapes and giant rock sculptures. While outsiders may think of it as a desert void, Navajos say there are no trees to block the beautiful view. The Four Corners is also home to one of America's most brilliantly colored landscapes.

This book is not laid out in straight lines and right angles. Like many galaxies and prehistoric symbols, it curves around itself in a spiral. Starting at the quadripoint, our path first takes us to the southwest, then north, east, south, west, and finally north again in a clockwise pattern.

A QUICK WORD ON TRAVEL ETIQUETTE

As you will see in this book, the Four Corners region is far different than anywhere else on Earth. And its people are distinct as well. They have unique customs, traditions, and patterns of acceptable social interaction—in other words, what is polite and proper etiquette.

In her book, *Native Roads: A Complete Motoring Guide to the Navajo and Hopi Nations*, Fran Kosik wrote a simple and insightful section titled "Travel Etiquette."

She says that among the Navajo, Hopi, and Paiute people, only medicine men are allowed to climb mountains because they are considered sacred places. Natives of Four Corners appreciate your respect for this, and they hope you will adapt their attitude of harmony and respect for nature as well. Visitors are also forbidden by the American Antiquities Act to remove prehistoric artifacts from federal lands, which includes Indian reservations.

Native peoples prefer that you ask their permission before including them in your photographs. While some do not want their pictures taken, others, especially in Canyon de Chelly and Monument Valley, generally receive a gratuity for acting as models. The Hopis prohibit all photography on their reservation, so it is best to leave your camera in the car.

On their website, www.experiencehopi.com/faq, the Moenkopi Legacy Inn has posted these rules about visiting the Hopi Villages:

» It is polite to accept invitations to eat, even if you eat or drink only a little.
» Alcohol is not allowed on Hopi or Navajo Tribal lands. Tribal law prohibits consumption.
» Pets are not allowed when touring Hopi land.
» Removal of pottery shards or rocks is prohibited.
» Sacred kivas (underground ceremonial chambers) and graveyards are off-limits.
» Please enter a home by invitation only.
» Public restrooms are not available.
» Dances are religious ceremonies; please refrain from clapping or taking pictures.

Appropriate dress is another sign of respect when visiting the Four Corners, especially when attending dances and other ceremonies. These are religious ceremonies and you should dress as you would when attending a wedding or baptism. Wear long pants or modest skirts instead of shorts, and definitely no tank tops, halter tops, or other immodest attire.

Part of the unique experience of visiting the Four Corners is in getting to know people who live and think differently and learning from these cultural encounters. This happens more fully when everyone is treated with friendship and mutual respect that results in rewarding new relationships.

1. Where Four States Meet

THE COLORADO PLATEAU

"You have to get over the color green; you have to quit associating beauty with gardens and lawns; you have to get used to an inhuman scale; you have to understand geological time."

—**WALLACE STEGNER**,
Where the bluebird sings to the lemonade springs: Living and writing in the West, 1955

The Colorado Plateau spans more than 150,000 square miles (390,000 sq km) from central Utah's Wasatch Mountain Range, north to the Uinta Range near Salt Lake City, to Colorado's Rocky Mountains in the east, and the Mogollon (moh-go-YONE) Rim in central Arizona to the south. The plateau's southern boundary has one of the most mispronounced names

Just south of the Utah-Arizona border, West Mitten and East Mitten loom over Monument Valley.

OPPOSITE: The Second Wave is similar to the nearby often-photographed "The Wave" in the Coyote Buttes section of the Paria Canyon-Vermilion Cliffs Wilderness Area.

in the region and is still called "Muggy-on" by many locals. The Colorado Plateau has an average elevation of 5,000 feet and is a semiarid high desert interspersed with high mesas, pinnacles, canyons, and rounded mountain ranges formed by molten rock. The winters are cold, summers are hot, and water is scarce.

One of the most interesting features of the Colorado Plateau is its remarkable geological stability. It has remained a thick block of the Earth's crust for more than 600 million years without the usual folding and faulting that has affected most other areas. For two billion years, while the Rocky Mountains and the Basin and Range regions were forming all around it, the four-mile-thick plateau eroded into a relatively smooth plane.

Beginning about four and a half million years ago (mya), the Earth's tectonic plates began to collide here, creating mountain ranges and canyons. At the same time, sediments sank to the bottom of prehistoric oceans, which dried out, the sediments hardened, and then the oceans came back, repeating the process for millions of years.

During the Paleozoic era, 542–251 mya, the supercontinent Pannotia broke up and Pangea formed as tropical seas periodically inundated the Colorado Plateau region. Thick layers of limestone, sandstone, siltstone, and shale were laid down in the shallow marine waters. When seas retreated, streams eroded older layers of sediment and deposited sands that piled into dunes. More than 300 million years passed as layer upon layer of sediment accumulated. What would eventually become today's Colorado Plateau broke away from the supercontinent Pangea 251 mya at the beginning of the Mesozoic era. The Me-

sozoic is divided into three periods: the Triassic (250–200 mya), the Jurassic (200–145 mya), and the Cretaceous (145–65 mya).

In the Early Triassic, the climate got warmer with less seasonal variation. Amphibians up to six feet in length left fossil footprints on stream bottoms in the Moenkopi Formation around Glen Canyon. Layers of sediment accumulated in short-lived lakes, ponds, streams, and inland seas and created the Chinle, Kayenta, and Moenave rock formations. After many centuries, the climate became subtropical, warm and humid. Jungle-like forests of palms and ferns grew abundantly along the banks of a vast muddy river that would later form a layer of shale.

Then in the Late Triassic, gigantic conifer trees as high as 250 feet fell and turned to stone in Arizona's Petrified Forest and the Glen Canyon National Recreation Area. Dinosaurs and early mammals appeared and evolved as the climate changed again in the Jurassic period. As the area heated and dried, dinosaur tracks were preserved in ancient dunes.

In another 100 million years, during the Late Cretaceous period, the climate changed again, with swamps forming along the coasts of another inland sea, forming sandstone, shale, and some coal deposits. The Cretaceous Seaway separated the western United States from the Great Plains. In this period, marine animals existed as indicated by their fossils in the Glen Canyon area, including oysters, mollusks, plesiosaurs, sharks, and skate. Then around 66 mya, at the end of the Cretaceous, about half of the vertebrates were killed off because of an asteroid six miles in diameter that crashed into what is now Mexico's Yucatán Peninsula.

More centuries passed. The area became an immense desert, and the Navajo and Temple Cap sandstone formations were created. The Laramide orogeny, a period of plate tectonic mountain building from 80 to 35 mya, closed the seaway and lifted up several blocks of the Earth's crust.

The most dramatic change occurred about 20 mya when the largest of these blocks, the Colorado Plateau, lifted straight up in one flat block about 1.8 miles (3 km). This raised streams—especially the Colorado, Green, San Juan, and Little Colorado—and they began to cut faster, eroding cliffs and widening basins. Up to this time, the Colorado River had meandered across a broad flat plain. As the plateau rose, the river began to run downhill with greater and greater force, eventually forming the Grand Canyon.

PREHISTORIC PEOPLES: FROM THE ICE AGE TO MULTISTORIED PUEBLOS

At the end of the last ice age, small groups of hunter-gatherers clothed themselves in fur, lived in caves, and made stone tools. In the 1920s and 30s, a particular type of stone tool was discovered near Clovis, New Mexico, dating from 12,500 to 10,000 BCE (Before Common Era). Named after the nearby town, these ancient people hunted some of the largest animals to ever roam the Earth: mammoths, giant ground sloths called *megatherium*, and Volkswagen-sized armadillos called *glyptodons*. Zoologists call them collectively *megafauna* (giant animals). In addition to stone tools, the Clovis people also worked with leather and bone tools and collected dozens of varieties of plants for food and clothing. After decades of excavations, most archeologists consider the Clovis Culture to be ancestors of most New World indigenous people.

During an interglacial period in the Holocene epoch ten thousand years ago, the climate became warmer and drier, which some scientists believe facilitated extinctions. However, humans with stone-tipped spears may have played a part in the megafauna's demise. By the time Homo sapiens grew to large numbers in the Southwest, the glyptodon and megatherium also faced extinction. Megafauna may have been weakened by climate-related factors like habitat loss, and then humans finished the job.

THE ANCESTRAL PUEBLOANS

From 10,000 to 500 BCE, a group of hunter-gatherers began to adapt. Archaeologists called them Anasazi for more than a century, but since that word means "Ancient Enemy" in Navajo, the Pueblo Indians formerly referred to their ancestors as "Ancient Ones" but now prefer that their ancestors be called Ancestral Puebloans. The Archaic-Early Basketmakers, the first stage of the Ancestral Puebloan culture, roamed the Colorado

Plateau hunting game and gathering wild plants. Small bands of people lived under rock overhangs and on the open plain in lean-tos and brush shelters. They dug hollows in the ground and made cone- or dome-shaped frames of branches or logs and covered them with brush and then plastered them with mud.

The Archaic-Early Basketmakers gradually changed from previous hunter-gatherer lifestyles by relying less on hunting large animals. Archaeologists believe that women harvested juniper berries and other fruit, grasses, mesquite beans, and nuts (in the baskets for which their culture is now named) in the spring, summer, and fall, and stored them during the winter months. In the fall and winter, the men hunted pronghorns, bighorn sheep, bison, and deer. They also invented a device called an *atlatl* to throw darts with small stone points. And they trapped rabbits and other small game.

Over the centuries, prehistoric farmers eventually outnumbered the hunter-gatherers. As early as 8,000 years ago, proto-farmers began helping the growth of wild plants like amaranth, wild grasses, mesquite beans, cactus fruit, and gourds by burning off unwanted foliage, weeding, irrigating, and replanting to ensure more growth.

About 2100 BCE, farmers in the Southwest began growing maize, centuries before crops were cultivated on the east coast. These farmers began to settle down and enlarge their communities.

The Ancestral Puebloans went through a major lifestyle change in the Early Basketmaker II Era (1500 BCE to 50 CE [Common Era]). They had been planting seeds in the spring and then continued their usual roaming to hunt and gather wild foods, returning to harvest their crops when they ripened. However, rodents, birds, and deer often devoured unattended crops, so they began to stay in one location to protect the harvest.

By the Late Basketmaker II Era (50–500 CE), the Ancestral Puebloans began to live in permanent pit houses, and started to fire pottery. This earthenware first appeared in the Southwest around 200 CE and spread throughout the Colorado Plateau by 500 CE.

Anthropologists divide earlier Ancestral Puebloan cultures into several "Basketmaker" stages because of their basket-making skills.

OPPOSITE: The Betatakin cliff dwelling at Navajo National Monument had 120 rooms that housed about 150 people.

INDIAN TRIBES OF THE FOUR CORNERS

NAVAJO

These Athapaskan speakers came from the Great Plains where they were hunter-gatherers, excellent horsemen, and raiders. They arrived in the Four Corners area sometime after 800 CE and settled next to the Pueblo people and learned to farm and make pottery from them. The Navajo people are a matrilineal society. At the center of Navajo culture is the concept of Hozho, the universal interconnection between beauty, harmony, and goodness in all things, both physical and spiritual. Respect for Hozho, including respect for their elders, results in health and well being for all living things and inanimate objects like rocks and stars as well.

The Navajo Nation is the largest Indian reservation in the United States, encompassing an area roughly 200 miles wide by 140 miles long in northeastern Arizona, southeastern Utah, and northwestern New Mexico. With a population of 356,890 members recorded by the 2016 U.S. Census, the Navajo are also the second largest tribe in the United States, next to the Cherokee. Navajo people are renowned for their silver and turquoise jewelry, rug weaving, healing sandpaintings, and sheep raising.

HOPI

These descendants of the Ancestral Puebloans, in what is now Arizona, speak a form of Uto-Aztecan and are experts at farming with very little water. Their spiritual beliefs are elaborate and complex with many gods and spirits including katsinam, represented in the dances and also in dolls carved from cottonwood tree roots. Several Hopi communities have maintained their ancestral culture and many Hopi are also known to be excellent runners.

UTE

The Ute are descended from hunter-gatherers who spoke the Numic language branch of Uto-Aztecan and migrated east from southern California to what is now Utah and Colorado around 1000 CE. The Ute call themselves Nuutsiu, "the people." Although it is still unclear, the name Ute may come from an Apache word for "people of the mountains" or "people of the north." The state of Utah gets its name from this tribe. Their language is similar to that of the Paiute, which indicates that they may have diverged hundreds, rather than thousands of years ago.

SOUTHERN PAIUTE

The Southern Paiutes are a subgroup of the Paiutes that established their homelands along the Colorado River in southern Nevada, southern Utah, and northern Arizona. They became more adapted to the desert environment while their relatives the Utes expanded their seasonal hunting trips into the Rocky Mountains where they adopted some cul-

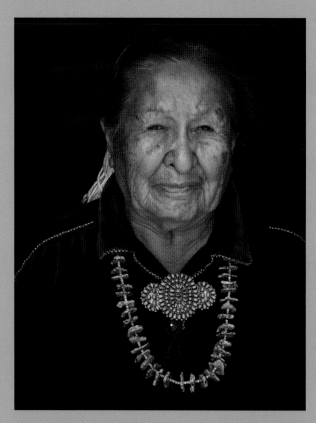

Turquoise jewelry, as worn by premier rug weaver Lucy Fatt, is a source of pride and tradition among the Navajo. TOP RIGHT: While traditional Hopi dances were only performed on their mesas, tribal groups outfitted in new regalia now perform in Flagstaff, Sedona, Mesa Verde National Park, and the National Museum of the American Indian in Washington D.C.

tural traits from the Plains Indians. The Southern Paiute are known for their traditional beadwork.

PUEBLO

These descendants of the Ancestral Puebloans live in villages called pueblos, the Spanish word for town or village. Like the Hopi, the Pueblo live in multistoried apartment-style homes modeled after their ancestors' great houses and cliff dwellings. The Pueblo people are divided into several distinct cultural groups, some of whom speak variations of a language called Keres or Keresan, while others speak Kiowa-Tanoan, a language related to Uto-Aztecan. The Pueblo are traditionally farmers but are also ranchers and known for their beautiful pottery. The general term *Pueblo Indian* refers to several federally recognized separate Indian tribes residing primarily in New Mexico.

LAGUNA

The Laguna people are a federally recognized Pueblo tribe who speak Western Keresan. Research of more than a thousand local archaeological sites indicates that people have been living in that area since 6,500 BCE. After the Pueblo Revolts (1680–1699) the Spanish founded a Catholic mission at the current location in 1699, naming the village Laguna because of a nearby lake created when prehistoric people built a dam there. At one time it was the only lake in what is now New Mexico.

ACOMA

The Acoma also speak Western Keresan and share cultural and religious ties with the Laguna people, including the Laguna-Acoma Jr.-Sr. High School located in between the two communities. The Acoma have a long tradition of creating beautiful pottery. While their traditional colors are orange and black on a white background, more recent generations of potters design with bright, vibrant colors. The geometric symbols on their pottery often represent rain, lightning, mountains, and the cycle of life.

ABOVE: Most Laguna pottery features abstract geometric designs but this water jar and other pieces depict more realistic animals and flowers. TOP RIGHT: Acoma pottery is renowned for its thin walls, fluted rims, and geometric designs.

ZUNI

The ancient Zuni village of Hawikuh was the first large Southwestern community to be visited by Europeans. Linguists note that the Zuni language is not related to any other language. Created about six thousand years ago, the Zuni language, or "Zuni Way," is spoken by only 9,500 people, some in Arizona but mostly around Zuni Pueblo, New Mexico. It is still the Zuni's primary language and most of their children speak it. The Zuni create beautiful pottery but are primarily known for their intricate petit point, needlepoint, fetish carving, and inlay jewelry traditionally made from coral, jet, mother of pearl, and turquoise stones.

Zuni dancers in traditional regalia performing the olla (water jar) dance.

Bows and arrows replaced the spear and atlatl during the Basketmaker III Era (500–750 CE). By this time, these people were living in complex pit houses, most of them near hunting grounds and fields.

By 750 CE, the Ancestral Puebloans began to build bigger houses. At first it was just rough lean-tos called *jacals*, wooden post frames covered with woven roofs and sides plastered with mud. Then stone slabs were propped up around a stone foundation.

Between 900 and 1150 CE, known as the Pueblo II Era, adequate rainfall and relatively warm temperatures allowed communities to reach peak population density and inhabit the settlements for longer spans of time. Pueblo II people developed specialized local architecture and pottery styles and began to domesticate turkeys and build irrigation canals, check dams, and terraces to adapt to seasonal rainfall conditions.

However, after several centuries of growth and improvement, around 1130 CE, several locations in the Western Hemisphere experienced what climatologists call the 300-year Great Drought. This affected their lifestyle dramatically, as will be seen at specific sites.

FOUR CORNERS MONUMENT

At first, several tribes, including Ute, Southern Paiute, Pueblo, and Navajo, inhabited the land where the four states now meet. The concepts of individual land ownership and legal boundaries arrived with the Spaniards in 1598, were perpetuated by the Republic of Mexico when they won their Independence in 1821, and continued via United States laws with the Treaty of

The official marker at the Four Corners Monument quadripoint. TOP: Pueblo Bonito in Chaco Canyon, New Mexico, was four to five stories high with more than eight hundred rooms.

Guadalupe Hidalgo in 1848.

The first common border line, between New Mexico Territory (which then included what is now Arizona) and Utah Territory, came with the Compromise of 1850. Then in 1861 Congress transferred some of Utah's land to the newly formed Colorado Territory. The new border between Utah and Colorado was the 32nd meridian west from the Washington (D.C.) Meridian, not the Greenwich Meridian (which became the standard reference point around 1912).

Although there was a brief Confederate Territory of Arizona, the U.S. Army's First California Volunteers drove the Confederates out of what is now Arizona in June of 1862, and in 1863 Congress made the split between Arizona and New Mexico territories on the north/south 32nd meridian, just like

Utah and Colorado, thus completing the quadripoint.

In 1875, the first surveying marker was placed showing the division of the territories, and a simple cement slab inscribed with the border intersection was constructed in 1912. A paved road made the monument accessible in 1962, and now each of the four states has its seal on the monument as well as the inscription, "Here Meet, in Freedom, Under God, Four States."

The monument area was rebuilt in 2009. Four Corners Monument is part of the Navajo Nation Parks and Recreation system and features a year-round visitors and demonstration center where Navajo artisans display their skills.

Several years ago the press made a big deal about how, according to the Global Positioning System (GPS) measurements, the current Four Corners Monument was in the wrong place as far as the official borders of each state are concerned, and that new GPS readings placed the monument 2.5 miles (4 km) off its mark. Officials from the National Oceanic and Atmospheric Administration's National Geographic Survey (NGS) responded with a technical report entitled "Why the Four Corners Monument is in Exactly the Right Place." The NGS then worked with the media to correct inaccuracies in their earlier stories, clarifying that the distance between the actual location of the monument and its intended location is not 2.5 miles as reported; the quadripoint is only 1,800 feet to the west of the marker. In addition, the NGS stated that a basic rule of boundary surveying is that once a monument has been established and accepted by all parties involved, it is the legal boundary, regardless of inaccurate measurements.

 ## 2. The Southwest Quadrant

TEEC NOS POS TRADING POST

About six miles south and a little west of the Four Corners Monument, you'll find one of the best traditional trading posts on the Navajo Reservation: Teec Nos Pos (rhymes with "lease toss loss") is Navajo for "cottonwood trees in a circle."

A native of Essex County, Virginia, Hambleton Bridger Noel came to Arizona to cure his tuberculosis in 1898. In 1905 he took a wagonload of goods to a favorite Navajo gathering spot and set up the area's first trading post amid a large stand of cottonwood trees in a canyon near the Carrizo Mountains very close to the quadripoint.

Noel married Eva Foutz in 1911. Her father, Joseph Lehi Foutz, came to Arizona with Mormon pioneer Jacob Hamblin in 1877 and managed or owned several trading posts on the Colorado Plateau. The Foutzes are related to the Tanners, another trading post dynasty. The post is now owned and managed by John McCulloch.

The original trading post burned to the ground in 1959, and the new post was built closer to U.S. Highway 160. "Teece," as locals call it, is an unassuming building on the outside, and

Wood carvings are one of many craft items available at trading posts for more than a century.

The earliest Navajo trade with non-natives was with Spanish settlers in the 1700s. Formal trading began with the Mormon settlements north and west of the Colorado River in the 1850s, but more Navajos moved to that area in 1862–63 as U.S. military campaigns against the Navajos began in earnest in New Mexico.

Early traders received government licenses and were allowed to build posts on Indian land without paying rent. The Navajos traded mostly for luxury items (like coffee and canned tomatoes) in those early days and so were not dependent on trade at that point.

When the majority of Navajos were sent to the internment camp at Bosque Redondo, many acquired a taste for Anglo goods, especially coffee, flour, salt, sugar, and canned goods, especially tomatoes. They learned the convenience of pots and pans, tools, bridles, and saddles. When the Navajos returned to Arizona after the Treaty of 1868, they were served by traveling traders who sold their goods out of wagons. By 1870, the market for Anglo goods was big enough that permanent trading posts opened to serve increased demands.

Toward the end of the nineteenth century, the number of trading posts increased in the Southwest. They were always owned and operated by non-Indians but often employed Indian managers. The trading post owners greatly increased Native arts and crafts production and its effect on the Native American economy. They supplied much-needed dry goods and food staples and provided Indians a market for their baskets, jewelry, rugs, sheep, and wool. When the railroad arrived in the Four Corners and made tourism travel easier, competition among post owners increased. Trading post owners and managers began to ask for products that were more likely to sell. Blankets gave way to rugs, smaller bracelets outsold big necklaces, and pottery creamers and salt and pepper shakers replaced pots as big-selling products.

inside it looks like a traditional general store except that it also has a butcher shop, jewelry counters, and all the jewelry and weaving supplies Navajos need to create their works of art. Teec Nos Pos is also the only buyer left for Navajo-raised raw wool and mohair on the Navajo Reservation.

And if that's not interesting enough, there's a room off to the side with a sign instructing you to wipe your feet before entering. Most trading posts call this the "Rug Room," and it is one of the best in the country. The walls and racks are covered with exquisite Navajo rugs of every style and design, and the cases and floors display traditional and contemporary wood-carvings, textiles, dolls, and all sorts of unexpected treasures.

SHEEPHERDING: A CULTURAL MAINSTAY

In 1598, Juan de Oñate brought Churro sheep to the upper Rio Grande Valley. For that reason, the Livestock Conservancy calls them "America's first domestic sheep." Churros are a hardy breed that adapt well to the Four Corners' scorching, dry desert heat to sub-zero temperature fluctuations. The breed now called "Navajo-Churro" has a double-coated fleece with a long staple (a naturally formed cluster or lock of wool), coarse outer coat that repels rain and snow while it protects their fine, soft inner coat from dust, dirt, and mud. The fleece is easy to work because it is low in grease, and the Churros come in a wide range of colors—blue, black, brown, red, silver, spotted, and white. And the Churros are known for the large number of rams born with four horns instead of the usual two.

The Churros were almost driven to extinction when the U.S. Army destroyed thousands of sheep and drove the Navajos to

Edward S. Curtis photographed these Yébîchai (grandfather or paternal gods) dancers in 1900. BELOW LEFT: While they weave, Navajo women watch their sheep and the baby in the cradleboard propped against the loom.

Bosque Redondo. During and after the Navajo internment, the U.S. Army issued the Navajos Merino sheep to raise. Merino wool is crimped, greasy, short, and hard to card and dye. This inferior wool, difficult to hand spin, was rejected by most Navajo weavers and they changed to commercially spun yarn. However, the sheep were still an important food source, and Navajos sold the wool to trading posts where it was shipped to textile mills.

The remaining Navajo-Churros were threatened again when government New Deal programs forced stock reduction sanctions in the 1930s. Today, the Navajo-Churro breed is still considered rare, but thanks to concerned breeders, the numbers are growing and there are enough to maintain a viable gene pool.

NAVAJO HISTORY, SACRED BELIEFS, AND CEREMONY

With a population of more than 173,000 living there and a land area of 27,096 square miles, the Navajo Nation is the largest United States Native American reservation. It covers parts of Arizona, New Mexico, and Utah. The Navajo Reservation is about the size of West Virginia, and covers the northern section of Arizona from Flagstaff to the New Mexico border.

Depending on whether you listen to traditions or anthropologists, the Navajos—who call themselves Diné (the people)—have either lived in the Four Corners area since coming up from a previous underground world, or they arrived from lands ranging from the Great Plains to Canada and Alaska, where other Athabaskan-speaking people still live. No one

knows how long ago the trek to their Southwestern homeland (Dinétah) began. Although scholars placed their arrival closer to 1500 CE, tree-ring dating (dendrochronology) places Navajo arrival as early as 1100 CE. (Dendrochronology compares the annual rings of tree limbs used in ancient buildings with more recent trees in order to gauge when the buildings were constructed. The dating process was refined by A. E. Douglass at the University of Arizona in the early 1900s.) Navajo legend places their arrival in the Chaco Canyon area between 900 and 1130 CE when the Ancestral Puebloans were leaving their pueblos. The word Navajo is the Spanish version of a Tewa (Pueblo group) word, *navaju*, which means "field" or "farm."

The Navajos hunted and farmed from Santa Fe, New Mexico, west to what is now Winslow, Arizona, and north to the Utah and Colorado state borders. They were semi-sedentary, with winter and summer homes combined with hunting and plant gathering trips. They found enough moisture in the dry land and sandy soil to grow corn, a process they learned from the Pueblo Indians.

The Navajo culture has remained intact mostly because many still live where their ancestors did, doing what they have done long before the Europeans arrived. Their history is the story of creating harmony with everything in the world. Right thinking, speaking, and planning create good living. According to their elders, the Navajos, came into this world from a previous one below in an area called El Gobernador Knob, near the San Juan River east of Farmington, New Mexico.

The gods and goddesses of Navajo beliefs explain the right way of living and how to maintain order and harmony. It all begins with the sun, followed by Changing Woman, who is known by many other names, such as White Shell Woman and Turquoise Woman. Changing Woman's home is in the west, but she changes her age and form when she passes through doors in the other directions of the compass. She gave the Diné the clouds, rain, pollen, dew, and prayer sticks.

First Man and Woman, who came from the previous world, asked the gods to create her. Entrance into the Fourth World (some say Fifth) became complete when Changing Woman was born. The Diné were all born from her, and she is Mother Earth. She represents the seasons and the phases of life. She

This 1904 Edward S. Curtis photograph of Navajos in Canyon de Chelly is considered one of his best.

The San Francisco Peaks are part of a volcanic range close to Flagstaff, Arizona. They hold considerable spiritual significance to thirteen American Indian tribes.

OPPOSITE TOP: Barboncito (1821–1871) was a great Navajo political and spiritual leader. He worked with another Navajo leader, Manuelito, to prevent forced relocation to Bosque Redondo.

grew from birth to puberty in four days and they had their first ceremony, now called Kinaalda, a Navajo rite of passage. She was given white shells, turquoise, abalone, and jet, and had to run toward the dawn for four days. The songs that were sung for Changing Woman are the ones that are still sung today for girls going through Kinaalda.

After that, Changing Woman met a stranger on the path several days in a row and learned that he was the inner personification of the sun. She bore him twins, who are most important to the Navajo people. Changing Woman has power over aging and rebirth, symbolizing the Earth's annual cycles, dying in the winter and reborn in the spring. She taught the Diné the songs for their ceremonies. Before she left the Navajo, she put them in charge of the Blessingway Ceremony and told them that if they forgot it, Navajo life would disappear. They were now responsible for keeping the world in perfect beauty and harmony.

The warrior twins, Monster Slayer and He Who Cuts Life Out of the Enemy, are as central to the Diné creation story as twins Damon and Pythias were to the ancient Greeks and Romulus and Remus to the Romans. Sometimes they fought monsters together, and other times Monster Slayer would go alone and his brother would stay home and pray for him. Just as real twins are said to do, He Who Cuts Life Out of the Enemy could sense when his brother was in trouble far away.

He Who Cuts Life Out of the Enemy, the younger twin, could shoot lightning bolts from his bow. He is the parent of all the waters. When his work was done and Changing Woman sent him away, she wept. When the twins were reunited in the sky, Monster Slayer wept joyfully. They agreed that they would always go together from then on, one doing the thinking and the other serving and protecting.

When her sons left, Changing Woman was lonely so she created four clans of humans by rubbing skin from her body. The clans went to the San Francisco Peaks near Flagstaff and spread out from there.

When all the monsters were slain, the Sun met Changing Woman at El Gobernador Knob and said he would build her a home in the west. At first she would not agree. She explained that she must have a beautiful house because he was of the sky, always in brightness, but she was of the earth and changed with the seasons. She told him that as different as they were, they were of one spirit and of equal worth. There can be no harmony in the world unless her requests mattered to him. The Sun built the house and gave her animals to take along so she wouldn't be lonely. The Sun visits her every night when his daily journey is done.

Even now there is still a god, or Ye'ii, whose body encompasses the area between the four sacred mountains, where all the Navajo people are safe.

THE EUROPEANS ARRIVE

"I hope to God you will not ask me to go to any other country but my own."
—BARBONCITO, Navajo Chief, May 1868

Although Francisco Vázquez de Coronado and his men visited Pueblo and Hopi villages briefly in their quest for the Seven Cities of Cibola in 1541–1542, there was no permanent European settlement in northern New Mexico for another fifty-six years. Then Don Juan de Oñate came from Mexico to set up a colony near present-day Santa Fe in 1598.

Several months later, twelve Spanish soldiers were killed at

Acoma Pueblo, known as the Sky City because of its lofty perch at the top of a 374-foot (114 meter) mesa. Oñate launched a retaliatory expedition of seventy Spanish soldiers, and on January 22, 1599, the Spaniards scaled the Acoma mesa and battled with the Pueblo Indians for two days. Approximately eight hundred Indians were killed and five hundred women and children, plus eighty warriors, were captured. The captives were either cut into pieces that were then thrown off the mesa, or were enslaved. The Spaniards cut off one foot of each adult male captive. Word spread quickly throughout the region that the Spaniards were their enemies, and some Pueblo people moved away from their ancestral villages.

After being punished by Spanish priests and imprisoned for practicing Native American religious ceremonies, Popé and other Pueblo Indian leaders moved to Taos Pueblo and spent the next five years planning a revolt. Tribes more than a hundred miles away, like the Zuni and the Hopi, pledged their support. Some Apaches and Navajos may have joined the battle as well. At the time, the Spanish population in northern New Mexico surrounding Santa Fe was about 2,400.

The attack began at Santa Fe on August 10, 1680. About four hundred Spaniards, *mestizos* (part Spanish, part Indian), and Indian servants, including twenty-one missionaries, women, and children, were killed. The 1,900 Spanish survivors fled to El Paso, returned in 1692, and after several more Native American revolt attempts, the Spaniards re-conquered the Puebloans by the end of the century. This Spanish *reconquista* (reconquest) had the effect of organizing the Navajos into a larger group with one leader, unlike the Apaches, who continued to live in small clan-based bands.

As Spanish conflicts eased after 1716, the Utes to the north began to raid into northwestern New Mexico. Now that the Navajos had cattle, sheep, and cotton cloth, and had settled more or less permanently, the Utes started raiding. Spanish ranchers moved next to the Navajos in the mid-1700s and they were welcome allies against the raiding Utes. But in 1773 the Spanish governor encouraged a war between the Utes and Navajos. The Navajos drove the Utes from the area the following year, and Governor Juan Bautista de Anza signed a treaty with the Navajos in 1786. These peaceful periods fostered a blending, or at least a cultural coexistence of Hispanics and Navajos.

Navajo expansion into Arizona grew at this time, and in 1805 nearly two decades of relative peace ended when Spaniards massacred hundreds of Navajo women and children during a slave raid in Canyon del Muerto in Canyon de Chelly,

Frederic Remington illustration of the 1540 Francisco Vázquez de Coronado expedition.

destroying any chance of lasting peace in the Four Corners. In retaliation, the Navajos began large-scale raids of Spanish settlements and by the 1820s the Navajos and Utes became Spain's most feared enemies.

Mexico won its independence in 1821 but fared even worse against the Navajos. With no royal treasury to back them up, reduced Mexican military forces were powerless over increased Navajo raiding for crops, livestock, and slaves. After Mexican independence, Navajos increased their livestock raids just as American merchants opened the Santa Fe Trail trade route from Missouri to New Mexico. This brought better guns for the Navajos, but the Mexicans still managed to capture hundreds of Navajos and other Native Americans and sell them into slavery.

New Mexico governor Manuel Armijo wrote in 1845, "the war with the Navajo is slowly consuming us." It is not surprising that Armijo surrendered his sword to Brigadier General Stephen Watts Kearny early in the Mexican-American War, handing the cultural conflicts over to the United States government.

Treaties and battles followed for the next seventeen years. Like the Apaches farther south, the Navajos thought they had won their war with the Euro-Americans when U.S. Army forts were closed and United States soldiers withdrew in 1861 because of the Civil War. Once the Confederate threat was gone by the fall of 1862, U.S. Brigadier General James H. Carlton resumed conflicts with the Navajos. He established Fort Sumner (previously known as Bosque Redondo) in northeastern New Mexico and planned to relocate the Navajos there. Some Navajo leaders accepted the offer to move, but Navajo leaders Barboncito and Manuelito refused to leave their ancestral homelands.

When the Navajos did not surrender on June 20, 1863 as ordered, General Carlton sent former fur trapper and scout Colonel Kit Carson and a thousand soldiers to Dinétah. Carson started a scorched-earth campaign, destroying Navajo orchards and cornfields and slaughtering thousands of sheep. More than 1,200 Navajos surrendered by February 1864, but many moved farther west.

The Navajos were sent to Bosque Redondo in February and March 1864. Called the Long Walk, it is considered the most traumatic event in Navajo history. About 8,500

John Gaw Meem/Library of Congress

Navajo Chief Manuelito (1818–1893) led his men in battles against other Navajos and Americans, but also signed several peace treaties, including the 1868 Treaty of Bosque Redondo that allowed the Navajo people to return to their homeland.

TONY HILLERMAN

No one captures the heart and soul of twentieth-century Four Corners like bestselling author Tony Hillerman. He was born in Sacred Heart, Oklahoma (population 50 in 1925), and his father was a farmer and storekeeper.

He dropped out of college in his first year to join the United States Army, took part in the D-Day Invasion in Normandy, and was awarded the Silver Star with Oak Leaf Cluster, Bronze Star, and Purple Heart for heroic actions and stepping on a land mine in France. But Hillerman said he got more from the war than just scars. He came back with self-confidence and self-respect, qualities he shares with his leading characters—quiet, unassuming lawmen just doing their jobs.

His first job when he got home was driving an oilrig supply truck in New Mexico. As it happened, on one of his deliveries he was allowed to attend a Navajo Enemy Way ceremony, which he described in his first book twenty years later. "I was impressed with their culture, which teaches Navajos to set aside anger, regret, bad memories and focus on the good," he said. Hillerman started at Oklahoma University on the G.I. Bill in 1946 and received a degree in journalism in 1948.

For the next twenty years he worked as a reporter and then editor for newspapers in New Mexico and Texas, then earned his master's degree in journalism in 1966 at the University of New Mexico, and taught journalism there for the next twenty years. He published his first novel, *The Blessing Way*, in 1970. A consistently best-selling author, his books have been translated into eight languages, including Japanese and Danish.

Hillerman introduced Lt. Joe Leaphorn of the Navajo Tribal Police in *The Blessing Way*, and Sgt. Jim Chee in *People of Darkness*, the fourth book in the series. Hillerman said that "Good reviews delight me when I get them but I am far more delighted by being voted the most popular author by the students at St. Catherine Indian School, and even more by middle-aged Navajos who tell me that reading my mysteries revived their children's interest in the Navajo Way."

Tony Hillerman's daughter Anne began writing the non-fiction book *Tony Hillerman's Landscapes: On the Road with Chee and Leaphorn* before her father's death and includes his comments. After he died in 2008, Anne continued the Chee and Leaphorn mysteries and won the Western Writers of America 2014 Spur Award for her *New York Times* best-selling novel, *Spider Woman's Daughter*.

men, women, and children were forced to trudge three hundred miles to Bosque Redondo, a place they called Hweeldi, which translates roughly as "the place of suffering." About two hundred died from frostbite, fatigue, and dysentery at Forts Wingate and Canby, or on the march itself, and several were abducted by slave traders along the way. Conditions were atrocious at Bosque Redondo. The lack of food and clothing, along with a shortage of wood to heat their hogans (traditional Navajo dwellings usually made of logs and earth), kept the Navajo in constant misery. In addition, more than 2,300 Navajos died from a smallpox epidemic, Kiowa Indian raids, and other causes.

In response to public outrage and reports from soldiers on duty there, a number of investigations were held. Finally, the Department of the Interior took over the situation from the Army on October 31, 1867. Early in 1868, Congress sent a Peace Commission to the Bosque Redondo Reservation. Barboncito told them, "I hope to God you will not ask me to go to any other country but my own." A treaty was signed, and on June 18 a ten-mile column of Navajos headed home. Navajo life would never be the same as it had been before the Long Walk. After Bosque Redondo, returning Navajos raised sheep and made blankets and jewelry to sell. By the 1880s, their livestock industry flourished.

NAVAJO NATIONAL MONUMENT

Go west on U.S. Highway 160 from Teec Nos Pos and then drive ten miles north on Arizona Highway 64 and you will find yourself at Navajo National Monument, home of Betatakin (ledge house) and Keet Seel (broken pottery), magnificent Ancestral Pueblo ruins. They are so big that you can see them from the path on the other rim of the canyon, and the ruins are well preserved because of their remote locations and because they are built into overhangs in a giant sandstone cliff, sheltered from the weather.

Facing a dense aspen grove and reached by a five-mile-long (8 km), challengingly steep walk, Betatakin is a multistoried pueblo of 135 rooms built beneath the overhanging wall of a huge wind cave that reaches five hundred feet in height. Construction of Keet Seel began in the 1240s, and Betatakin was constructed about forty years later.

CANYON DE CHELLY

Six miles east of Chinle, Arizona, layers of Permian-age sandstone, primarily De Chelly Formation, were laid down 200 million years ago. Then the Rio de Chelly flowed its serpentine course westward from the Chuska Mountains into the Chinle Wash, while wind and weather joined to carve canyons with looming 1,000-foot-tall walls. Spider Rock, the most impressive formation in the monument, rises 750 feet (229 m) straight up from the canyon floor.

Keet Seel sits on a remote cliff ledge in Navajo National Monument, Arizona. OVERLEAF: About 150 people lived at Betatakin before drought probably caused its abandonment after less than fifty years of habitation.

The name Chelly is a Spanish translation of the Navajo "Tsegi" or "Tséyi" (rock canyon). Over several centuries, the original pronunciation "de shay-yee" has been shortened to "d'Shay." Canyon de Chelly became a national monument in 1931, but unlike all other U.S. national monuments, the Navajo Nation retains ownership of the land.

Humans have prospered in Canyon de Chelly for more than five thousand years, making it one of North America's most continuously inhabited places. It was home to the Archaic people, the Basketmakers, the Ancestral Puebloans, the Hopis, and now the Navajos. There are more than eight hundred archaeological sites in the area. The Navajos still farm and raise livestock below ancient cliff dwellings.

According to National Park Service researchers, between 1749 and 1753, groups of mixed Navajo/Pueblo ancestry moved from the Spanish missions in western New Mexico to northeastern Arizona because of drought and Ute raids.

In 1853, after the area became part of the United States, Indian Agent Henry Dodge reported abundant crops in the area, including superior quality peaches. Conflicts between Ute Indians, Navajos, and U.S. soldiers continued through the end of the decade.

Rising 750 feet (229 meters) above the canyon floor, Spider Rock is a spiritual touchstone for Native Americans and visitors alike. OPPOSITE: Occupied from 1060–1275 CE, the trail to White House Ruin is the only one that visitors can take into Canyon de Chelly without a permit or authorized Navajo guide.

During the Civil War, Union volunteers from Colorado, New Mexico, and California drove the Confederates out of New Mexico, and in January 1864, Colonel Carson's forces destroyed crops and livestock in Canyon de Chelly and drove five hundred Navajos into confinement at Bosque Redondo. The Navajos returned in 1868 and still raise sheep, horses, and crops in the canyon.

DINÉ COLLEGE

Twenty-five miles from the Canyon de Chelly National Park visitor center, at the far northeast end of the canyon, at Tsaile, Arizona, you will see a beautiful six-story, eight-sided building with mirrored-glass facings. This architectural wonder opened in 1968 as the first tribally controlled community college in the United States. There are eight fifteen-room dormitories surrounding the main building and each of these eight-sided units has a fireplace in the center and was described in college literature as a "hooghan away from hogan," a home away from home. Courses vary from traditional business administration, computer science, and mathematics, to Navajo language and Diné studies. There are also seven other branches to serve the Navajo Nation.

LUKACHUKAI, ARIZONA

Ten miles north of Diné College and about a mile east of Indian Route 12, you will find the community of Lukachukai, population 1,700. The name means "land of white reeds" in Navajo. Nestled beneath the shady green Chuska Mountains, the grass grows tall there and even in the driest of years, water leaps from the ground at Waterfall Spring.

CHINLE, ARIZONA

The Navajo people call this area Ch'ini'li which means "where the water flows out" to describe the location of the water flowing out from Canyon de Chelly. The first tent-style trading post opened in 1882 and it grew to a full-sized post over the next three years. With a population of 4,518 in 2010, three motels, several gas stations, and even a shopping center, Chinle is the gateway to Canyon de Chelly National Monument.

GANADO, ARIZONA

Forty miles southwest of Canyon de Chelly, the Ancestral Pueblo people found the Pueblo Colorado River (also known as Pueblo Colorado Wash) an excellent place to farm. The Basketmakers may have grown crops there as early as 1800 BCE and the flowing streams and accessible terrain allowed for an ancient trade-route crossroads. The area was probably abandoned for centuries until the Navajos began to settle there in the mid-to-late-nineteenth century.

In 1858, Lieutenant Joseph Christmas Ives visited the Pueblo Colorado Wash that runs through what is now Ganado. "We found a pretty creek running between steep earth banks ten or twelve feet high. The water is good though warm. . . . Countless herds of horses and flocks of sheep were grazing upon the plain." The future town of Ganado had several things going for it. It was near a good water source and at a crossroads of several Navajo communities. It was just south of the Navajo Reservation boundary, and therefore good for Anglo traders too.

The 2010 U.S. Census counted 1,210 people living in Ganado. Today, Ganado is one of the leading Navajo Nation communities. A board of local farming advocates manage farmlands, organic beef and mutton are raised at surrounding ranches, there are satellites of Diné College and Northern Arizona University, and Sage Memorial Hospital serves thousands of Hopi and Navajo patients.

Hubbell Trading Post hosts a yearly art show in late summer that includes displays of paintings, drawings, sculptures, jewelry, rug weaving and other art forms. The Ganado Rodeo Club also hosts events.

HUBBELL TRADING POST

Good night. It is scribbled on the panels
of the cold gray open desert.
Good night; on the big sky blanket over the
Santa Fé trail it is woven in the oldest
Indian blanket songs.

—CARL SANDBURG, *Slabs of the Sunburnt West*, 1922

Ganado is best known as the location for one of the most renowned trading posts in the Four Corners, the Hubbell Trading Post. John Lorenzo Hubbell, the man the post is named after, was born in Parajito, New Mexico, in 1853. His father was James Hubbell, a Connecticut Yankee who came to New Mexico as a soldier during the Mexican-American War in 1846. James married Juliana Gutiérrez, granddaughter of New Mexico's governor. John Lorenzo was a sutler's clerk at Fort Wingate, and in 1874 a Navajo Indian Agent hired Hubbell (who was fluent in Spanish and passable in Navajo) to work with Navajo leader Ganado Mucho to settle some disputes. Ganado Mucho lived in the Pueblo Colorado Valley and may have influenced Hubbell's choice to start a business there.

William B. Leonard and his partner Barney Williams arrived in 1875 and built a post on the site of the current Hubbell Trading Post. John Lorenzo Hubbell arrived in 1876 and started trading near Ganado Lake but then bought Leonard's place in 1878. Soon after, "Don Lorenzo" Hubbell changed the name of the settlement from Pueblo Colorado to Ganado to honor his friend Ganado Mucho and to avoid confusion with another town named Pueblo in Colorado, which became a state in 1876.

"The Hubbell" is the longest continuously operating post in the Four Corners area. The Hubbell family ran the enterprise until 1967 when the federal government purchased it and created Hubbell Trading Post National Historic Site. It is still open for Navajos who come in to trade for supplies, but is now run by the non-profit Western National Parks Association.

KEAMS CANYON TRADING POST

Lók'a'deeshjin, a Navajo word meaning either "reeds extend in a black line" or "black reeds in the distance," was originally a farming area in a deep sandstone canyon near the Hopi village of Polacca.

The location was also formerly known as Peach Orchard Springs. Now called Keams Canyon, it took its new name from Thomas Varker Keam, born in Kenwyn, England in 1842. He served in the British and then American military. Keam received his honorable discharge from the U.S. Army at Santa Fe, New Mexico, in 1868. He then received an Indian Bureau license to trade with the Indians.

Keam married Grey Woman in a traditional Navajo cere-

The Hubbell Trading Post looks much the same as it did more than a century ago.

mony and was appointed as a temporary special agent to the Navajos in 1872. He partnered with William Leonard and established what would be known as Keams Tusayan Trading Post in 1879. Its location forty-four miles west of Ganado and just a few miles east of First Mesa allowed Keam to trade with both Navajos and Hopis, and he learned both their languages. The Bureau of Indian Affairs bought his property in 1886 and Keam moved his post about a quarter mile west to the mouth of the canyon, where Keams Canyon shopping center stands today, part of which now operates as McGee's Indian Art Gallery.

THE HOPI WORLD

The majority of the Hopi people live on three mesas, uncreatively named by European explorers east to west as First Mesa, Second Mesa, and Third Mesa. They are all outcroppings of the southern edge of Black Mesa. Known as Dziłíjiin (Big Mountain) in Navajo, Black Mesa is a mountainous region between Tuba City and Chinle and reaching almost to Monument Valley to the north. It rises to 8,168 feet at its high point, and all roads go to the north or south of the mesa to get around it. Black Mesa gets its name from the seams of coal that provide fuel for the Navajo Generating Station at Page, Arizona.

Old Oraibi on Third Mesa is one of the four original villages. Recent scholarship sets the founding between 1200 and 1250 CE, making it one of the oldest continuously inhabited villages in the United States. The Hopi Cultural Center and Hotel is on Second Mesa along with the villages of Shungopavi, Sipaulovi, and Mishongnovi.

There are four villages on First Mesa including the historic village of Walpi, known for its high-rise dwellings with panoramic views of beautiful sunsets. The villagers on all three

WEAVING FOR THOUSANDS OF YEARS

Anthropologists believe that Native Americans began weaving with plant fibers more than five thousand years ago. The Navajos say that Spider Woman taught Changing Woman how to weave, and she then passed on the craft to all Navajo women. Spider Man made the first loom and weaving tools out of turquoise, jet, white shell, and abalone. Weaving is an important part of Navajo spiritual beliefs, and there are some taboos involved in this sacred activity. Some do not include images of bears or holy ones (Ye'ii) in their designs. Many still leave a spirit trail, or weaver's pathway, through the border when finishing a rug.

Many Navajo girls learn how to weave from their mothers or grandmothers before they are ten years old. For many Navajo women, weaving is the center of their life, their family, and their community. Because their looms are portable, women can tend sheep, watch their children, and weave simultaneously. Their art is a matter of personal pride, and weavers are well respected by the Navajos.

In the middle of the seventeenth century, after the Spaniards colonized New Mexico, Navajos learned how to herd sheep and process wool. Pueblo men had been weaving cotton blankets as early as 800 CE, and by the late 1700s the Navajos learned how to weave from them. They sometimes intermarried, and the Pueblo men most likely taught their Navajo wives how to weave.

The Navajos became the best weavers in the West, and Navajo blankets were prized by the other Indian tribes and Spanish alike. They were traded to the Sioux, Cheyenne, and Ute, and were valued because the tight weave was almost waterproof. They were also much lighter than buffalo robes for use as coats by day and bedding by night.

Their Classic Period high-quality weavings were called chief's blankets because they were so expensive that only chiefs and other wealthy people could afford them. From the 1820s to about 1865, "First Phase" Chief's blankets were simple red, blue, and brown stripes. In the decades that followed, weavers added rectangles (also called bars) to their designs. Diamond and triangle shapes followed, then crosses and thin lines. Aniline dyes derived from coal tar replaced indigo and cochineal in the 1870s. Trading posts supplied dye packets that increased the color choices, including green and yellow, but the favorite was still dark red because it represents spiritual life.

In the 1870s, John Lorenzo Hubbell got a lot pickier about the quality and design of the blankets he would accept in trade. He would not buy cotton warp rugs, which didn't last as long, and discouraged bright colors, persuading weavers to use natural wool colors plus deep-red-dyed wool. Most of the early "Ganado Red" rugs feature terraced diamond and triangle motifs, now adding black, brown, grey, or white accents, usually sticking with single or double triangles with corner triangle designs.

Hubbell hung Anglo artists' hand-painted examples of earlier blankets on his walls. But times changed, and even his design refinements did not save the blanket trade from what came with the railroad. By the 1880s, the Santa Fe Railway brought tourists by the thousands to the Southwest. This meant a business boom for the Navajos, but Americans wanted floor rugs instead of blankets. Meanwhile, the Pendleton Woolen Mills began making Indian-pattern blankets in 1896, and charged $3 for a patterned blanket as opposed to $100 for an original Navajo product.

Navajo weaving is still thriving in the Four Corners, and one of the best places in the world to buy rugs is the Crownpoint Rug Auction. Started fifty years ago and now managed by the Navajo Rug Weavers Association of Crownpoint, the event usually takes place on the second Friday of the month at the Crownpoint Elementary School, sixty miles northeast of Gallup, New Mexico. Dates are listed on their website: http://crownpointrugauction.com/

A rainbow lands on Walpi, First Mesa. Long vistas provide excellent views around the Hopi country.

OPPOSITE LEFT: Located twenty miles southeast of Tuba City, Coal Mine Canyon is a series of ravines filled with multicolored spires, cliffs, and weather-sculpted sandstone formations.

mesas are noted for crafting katsina dolls, fine traditional woven clothing, coiled baskets, paintings, drawings, and turquoise and silver overlay jewelry, but most Hopi pottery is created on First Mesa.

There were more than 7,500 Hopis in the United States in 2015, according to the U.S. Census. Their language is one of thirty Uto-Aztecan language subgroups spoken from Idaho to El Salvador. The Hopi people call their ancestors *Hisatsinam*, known to anthropologists as Ancestral Puebloans. The name Hopi has been shortened from Hopituh Shi-nu-mu, and can be translated as "The Peaceful People." In a deeper sense, it means "one who is mannered, civilized, peaceable, polite, and adhering to the Hopi Way," according to the *Hopi Dictionary*.

The Hopi Way is to strive toward reverence and respect for all things. Hopis believe that their ceremonies benefit the whole world. They believe the land is sacred, and agriculture is an important part of their livelihood and culture. They are highly skilled micro or subsistence farmers, able to sustain crops on very little water.

At the center of the Hopi Way is the katsina (formerly

known as kachina). To the Hopi, Zuni, Tewa, Acoma Pueblo, and Laguna Pueblo people, katsinam (plural) are benevolent spirit beings or personifications of antelope, corn, insects, snow, sun, thunderstorms, wind, and many other concepts in the real world and central to their spiritual life. There are more than four hundred types of katsinam in the Hopi and Pueblo pantheon, and katsinam exist in three aspects. They can be spiritual beings, or masked dancers in religious ceremonies, or, as they are most well known, carved wooden dolls given to children to teach them about the various spirits they represent and how the universe works. Katsinam have the power to help humans by healing, bringing rain, or protecting them from adversity. They show that life resides in all things in the universe, and that humans must be in harmony with them all. The Hopis believe that the katsinam live on the San Francisco Peaks near Flagstaff.

The Hopi Reservation encompasses 2,532 square miles (8,557 sq km) but the land has been disputed with the surrounding Navajo Nation for many decades. The U.S. Congress passed acts in 1974 and 1996 to apportion lands on which both tribes lived. However, not all the families living in the other tribe's area have moved, and as of this writing land ownership is still in controversy.

TUBA CITY: WHEN IS A CITY NOT A CITY?

According to most geographers, settlements of 100,000 to 3,000,000 people are considered cities, large cities, or metropolises. But Tuba City, population 8,611 in the 2010 United States Census, has never seemed to care for the rules. Slightly larger than Shiprock, New Mexico, it is the Navajo Nation's largest community.

Hopi farmers from Oraibi built the village of Moenkopi a few miles southeast of Tuba City around 1870 and grew large cotton crops in the Moenkopi Wash's rich soil. Mormon pioneer Jacob Hamblin blazed trails in Utah and northern

Arizona as early as 1858 and met Hopi headman Tuuvi twenty years later. Tuuvi converted to Mormonism and the Mormons named their settlement after the Hopi leader (whose name they evidently mispronounced and misspelled) and optimistically added "City."

The Navajo name for Tuba City is Tó Naneesdizí, "tangled waters," for the many underground springs that form reservoirs there. The water attracted Hopis and Paiutes to settle there, but most of the current residents are Navajo.

Located in the center of town on Main Street, the Tuba City Trading Post was established in 1870, and in 1905 Flagstaff's pioneering Babbitt brothers took ownership and designed the two-story cut-stone building with eight sides just like a Navajo hogan. The restored trading post, now owned and operated by Navajo Nation Hospitality Enterprise, is well stocked with a wide variety of Native American arts and crafts as well as Southwestern clothing.

There are two museums just a few steps from the trading post. The Explore Navajo Interactive Museum, whose ultra-modern geodesic dome design also replicates the hogan shape, was built as an exhibit for the 2002 Winter Olympics in Salt

LOUIS TEWANIMA, HOPI RUNNER

Bain News Service/Library of Congress

Most Hopi people have chosen to live in their own world, geographically, socially, and spiritually. More than a century ago, however, there was one Hopi man who became internationally famous. That man was Louis Tewanima, silver medalist in the 10,000-meter run in the 1912 Summer Olympics in Stockholm, Sweden.

Born in 1888, Tewanima and his friends liked to run the sixty miles from Second Mesa to Winslow when they were kids. He was sent first to the boarding school at Fort Wingate and then to Carlisle Indian School where his track coach was Glenn "Pop" Warner, a famous American football coach.

Louis Tewanima ran the marathon in the 1908 Olympics in London and the Boston Marathon in 1909. After wins in the 1920s from New Orleans to New York City, sportswriters nicknamed him "the fastest man in the world." He didn't appear to be affected by his fame and returned to Second Mesa to grow corn and raise sheep. Tewanima was selected for the all-time U.S. Olympic track and field team in 1954 and inducted into the Arizona Sports Hall of Fame in 1957. He died in 1969 at age eighty-seven when his eyesight failed him while returning home one night after a ceremonial dance and he fell from a seventy-foot cliff.

In 1974 the Hopi people created the Louis Tewanima Footrace in his honor. Held on Sunday during the Labor Day weekend, the 10k and 5k courses start at the top of Second Mesa and follow a foot trail that circles around and down through a riverbed and ends with a climb up a steep stone staircase back to the top of the mesa and the finish line. The race is open to all, and many leading runners attend.

Lake City, Utah. The door is on the east, just like a hogan, and visitors travel clockwise inside the circular building, which is divided into four sections that suggest the four cardinal directions and the four seasons. The four museum sections, which describe the Navajos' lifetime journey, are land, language, history, and culture and ceremonial life. Admission includes entry to the Navajo Code Talkers Museum in the back part of the Tuba City Trading Post. Actual gear and tools used in battle, plus excerpts from Code Talker memories and detailed photographs depict the fascinating story of patriotic Navajos who used their language to create an unbreakable code that helped win World War II.

JURASSIC DINOSAUR TRACKS

About five miles west of Tuba City you can see the world's only "running dinosaur" tracks, left in the mud and then fossilized in sandstone two hundred million years ago. The skeletal remains of *Dilophosaurus* were found just a few hundred yards away from these dinosaurs' three-toed tracks near Tuba City. They walked on two legs and had two smaller arms, like the *Tyrannosaurus* rex, which would come along about 130 million years later. *Dilophosaurus* gets its name from the two thin crests of bone on top of its skull. They ranged up to twenty-three feet long, stood up to twenty feet tall when fully upright, and weighed about half a ton (453 kg).

Dilophosaurus was one of the cloned stars in the 1993 blockbuster, *Jurassic Park*. However, it is highly unlikely that the real-life version had expandable multicolored fans sprouting from its crest or shot venom at its victims. Smaller tracks in the area are attributed to *Coelophysis*, a more slender nine-foot-long theropod (Greek for "wild beast," and characterized by hollow bones and three toes, like birds).

KAYENTA, ARIZONA

Artist Maynard Dixon said it was "a damn long ways in any direction, from anywhere." But somehow some of the most talented people felt the need to visit Kayenta in the early twentieth century. A few all-time great Western artists, including Carl Oscar Borg and Maynard Dixon, stayed at the Kayenta Trading Post, and several cartoonists showed up too. Rudolph Dirks (*the Katzenjammer Kids*), George Herriman (*Krazy Kat*), and Frank King (*Gasoline Alley*) illustrated the Kayenta guest books with scenes of their characters frolicking in Monument Valley.

There's an intermittent spring there that led to the town's Navajo name, *Tódinéeshzheé* (water spreading out like fingers). The population was 5,189 in 2010, and it is a convenient overnight stop for tourists on their way to Monument Valley Tribal Park twenty-five miles to the north.

Beside Route 160 in Kayenta, you can visit the Navajo Cultural Center, a two-acre park that has several examples of different types of hogans and, most important, a replica of a Navajo shade house that contains a large collection of Navajo Code Talker artifacts curated in excellent exhibits presenting the history of the Code Talkers and information on Navajo be-

Up close, Church Rock seems like it belongs on a different planet. Agathla Peak can be seen ten miles (16 kilometers) in the distance. LEFT: Dinosaur tracks! Just one more thing that makes the Four Corners area fascinating.

liefs and traditions. Navajo entrepreneur Richard Mike created the Cultural Center. His father, King Mike, was a Navajo Code Talker and mailed back or brought home the artifacts displayed as well as some photographs and smaller three-dimensional items displayed in the Burger King next door, also owned by the Mike family.

AGATHLA PEAK

East of U.S. Route 63 between Kayenta and Monument Valley, a giant black rough-hewn "volcanic plug" juts up from the plateau. This pinnacle is Agathla Peak, which the Navajos believe is the center of the universe. Agathla is a rough translation of the Navajo word that means "much wool," and it was named for animal fur found around the base of the peak. Colonel Kit Carson named it "El Capitan" in the 1860s because of its imposing presence. Agathla Peak rises as much as 1,500 feet (457 m) above the sandstone plateau.

Although other cultures have also painted with sand, Navajo sandpaintings are both artistic and spiritual creations. TOP: Although the Spaniards named it "El Capitan," most references prefer Agathla, for what Navajos consider the center of the universe.

Many things make Four Corners seem like a completely different world, but sandpaintings top the list for their unique media and design. In a land where the rocks and sand have not changed for millions of years, the Hopi, Pueblo, and Navajo people create ephemeral works of art right on the ground using dirt, powdered chalk, charcoal, leaves, sand, ground turquoise, other minerals, pollen, and cornmeal. Sometimes called dry paintings, these spiritual tools are used in Navajo ceremonies to treat illness, bestow blessings, drive out evil, and restore harmony to the world.

A Navajo *hataali* (singer/medicine man) and perhaps one or two apprentices draw the paintings on the floor of a hogan using exact traditional designs of supernatural beings with powers to change the elements. Usually created in less than a day, the paintings are used in a nighttime ceremony and then a stick adorned with feathers is used to destroy the painting.

Although specific sandpaintings shouldn't be seen by anyone other than the patient and healers, anthropologists and traders began reproducing them in the late 1800s to record the knowledge. In 1923, architect Mary Elizabeth Jane Colter used sandpainting motifs at the Harvey Company's Hotel Navajo in Gallup, New Mexico. Some Navajo artists take part in the Blessingway ceremony before creating this type of replica and believe that changing the images, colors, or composition removes any ill effects of producing permanent sand art images outside the spiritual context.

OVERLEAF: The red sands, bluffs, and spires of Monument Valley.

MONUMENT VALLEY

"My first sight of Monument Valley came with a dazzling flash of lightning. It revealed a vast valley, a strange world of colossal shafts and buttes of rock, magnificently sculptured, standing isolated and aloof, dark, weird, lonely."

—ZANE GREY, "Nonnezoshe—The Rainbow Bridge," *The Recreation Magazine*, February, 1915

Today, almost everyone in the world has seen images of the fantastic sandstone formations at Monument Valley, even though it is not on the way to anywhere and more than a hundred miles from interstate freeways. Its remoteness is part of its character and also the reason it didn't receive any attention until the early 1900s when magazine articles and movies shared Monument Valley with the world.

At first only a handful of explorers, adventurers, and tourists came to the area. But when it became the base for explorations to Rainbow Bridge (forty-three miles to the west over rugged terrain) and the public read and saw pictures of the area, Monument Valley became a major attraction.

In 1910, the Wetherills moved thirty miles south from Oljato to Kayenta. It was a day closer to their supply line, and they built a trading post there in the spring of 1911. In 1915, Zane Grey wrote a sequel to *Riders of the Purple Sage* (considered to be the most popular Western novel of all time) called *The Rainbow Trail*, and the main characters were based on John and Louisa Wetherill.

Petroglyphs at Eye of the Sun Arch, Monument Valley.

By 1913 there was a new industry and a different group of visitors: the moving picture people. Zane Grey demanded that movies based on his novels must be filmed in the actual locations, so the cameras followed him to the Four Corners.

In 1925 *The Vanishing American* became the first movie filmed in Monument Valley. From then on, the Wetherills were in the movie business, providing mule teams and lodging for the moviemakers.

But now there was a new couple in the area, right in the center of Monument Valley. They were Harry and Leone Goulding, destined to serve the movie industry for almost four decades. Harry Goulding was a true Westerner, born in Durango, Colorado in 1897. He came from a family of sheep ranchers, and when Leone Knee first saw Harry at the American Hotel in Aztec, New Mexico, she said he was a tall lanky wrangler in boots, Levi's, and a cowboy hat. They got married in 1923 when she was 18 and he was 26. He had a hard time spelling her name when he wrote to her, so he just called her Mike.

The young couple then set off on an adventure and forty-five-year romance in Monument Valley. The land that straddled the Utah/Arizona border had belonged to the Paiute tribe, but the United States government swapped them for more fertile land farther north in order to open the area for oil exploration. When oil prospects fizzled and the land was open for homesteading, Harry sold his Colorado ranch and purchased 640 acres at the base of Big Rock Door Mesa.

At first the situation was tense with the Navajos and Paiutes, but the Native people soon realized that goods they wanted were now thirty miles closer. Harry Goulding began buying sheep in Monument Valley a few years earlier so the Navajos called him Dibé Nééz— "Tall Sheep." They liked him because he was generous, cooperative, and he extended their store credit in rough times.

Harry and Mike lived in a 10 × 12-foot tent for two years until they could build a stone building for living quarters and a trading post. Harry began raising sheep, but severe droughts in 1934 and 1936 led him to find another income source.

Harry went to Hollywood in the 1930s and came home with contracts. Monument Valley would not be the Western icon it is today if it hadn't been for Harry Goulding and photographer Josef Muench. Muench was born in Schweinfurt, Bavaria, in 1904 and immigrated to Detroit when he was 24. His first pic-

ture of Rainbow Bridge appeared in *Arizona Highways* in 1938, and later Muench said he visited Monument Valley 160 times during his sixty-year career.

Harry Goulding said he learned that United Artists wanted to film a Western on location somewhere in the West. He asked his friend Muench to put together an album of Monument Valley photographs to showcase its beauty and grandeur. Then in 1938 Harry and Mike drove right to United Artists headquarters in Hollywood. The story goes that when Harry couldn't get past the receptionist, he threatened to bring in his bedroll and camp out in the office. Whether he did or not, a location manager for the upcoming movie *Stagecoach* saw the pictures and

then director John Ford looked at them. Later, Ford said that it wasn't the first time he'd heard of Monument Valley.

But the photos and Harry's enthusiasm must have sold Ford on the location because Harry said he left the office with a check for $5,000. Ford made six more films in Monument Valley over the next twenty-five years and said that Monument Valley was the "most complete, beautiful, and peaceful place on earth."

Monument Valley is a combination of siltstone, sandstone, and shale sparsely dotted with desert-hardy juniper and yucca plants. The striking monuments of Monument Valley continue to be created as soft shales of the Cutler Formation erode away, leaving massive, vertically jointed slabs of De Chelly Sandstone without support. Both formations are from the Permian geologic period, 298–252 million years ago.

Organized similar to America's national parks, in 1958 the Navajo tribal government voted to set aside 29,817 acres (120.66 sq km) as Monument Valley Navajo Tribal Park. The tribe earmarked $275,000 for road upgrades and a visitor center. They literally paved the way for other Native Americans to design similar tourist recreation areas. The park attracts about half a million visitors a year from all over the world.

RAINBOW BRIDGE NATIONAL MONUMENT

"I had a strange, mystic perception that this rosy-hued, tremendous arch of stone was a goal I had failed to reach in some former life, but had now found."

—ZANE GREY, *Tales of Lonely Trails*, 1922

Rainbow Bridge is often described as one of the world's highest natural bridges. In 1974 the United States Bureau of Reclamation reported the bridge's span to be 275 feet (84 m), but a 2007 laser beam measurement amended that to 234 feet (71 m). The Statue of Liberty could be tucked under the Rainbow Bridge with room to spare.

In the late Cretaceous period (110–66 mya), ancient seas moved east across the Colorado Plateau and ran into landmasses moving west, which created large barriers and mud flats, creating new sandstone formations—Dakota, Mancos Shale, and the Mesa Verde Group. At the same time, a series of orogenies, geological events where overlapping tectonic plates grind together, caused folding and faulting, creating mountains, and the intense friction melted solid rock into magma and forced it toward the surface where it often erupted into volcanoes. Seventy to eighty million years ago during the middle Tertiary period, the Laramide orogeny moved the entire Colorado Plateau upward more than five thousand feet.

Near the current Arizona/Utah border about 65 million years ago, a large body of magma bulged almost to the surface but did not break through at ground level, forming what is now called Navajo Mountain. Magma bulges like this are called laccoliths, differing from volcanoes in that there are no lava beds, volcanic debris, or cinder cones surrounding them, and they are usually smooth domes. After the great dome pushed skyward to more than 10,000 feet above modern sea level, water flows in the area intensified and erosion increased.

Then thirty million years ago, during the middle Tertiary period, the Colorado River and its tributaries started slicing through 5,000 feet of sedimentary rock, the dried remains of ocean beds that had been pushed up by tectonic actions. As the cuts got deeper over thousands of years, more and more water

LOUISE WADE WETHERILL

Louise Wade Wetherill's passion for Navajo culture attracted artists and scientists alike. Usually known as Louisa, she often minded the store while her husband John was away freighting goods or leading expeditions. The Navajos called her Ashton Sosi, Slim Woman. She spoke Navajo and knew their beliefs and customs well.

A true pioneer woman, Louisa Wade was born in 1877 in Nevada to United States Army Captain Jack Wade and his wife Julia France Rush Wade. The family moved to Mancos, Colorado, at about the same time as their neighbors, the Wetherills, began ranching there. Louisa married John Wetherill in 1896, and in the next few years Benjamin and Georgia Ida were born. They began managing trading posts in New Mexico in 1900 at Ojo Alamo (near Chaco Canyon) and Chavez, then Richard and John Wetherill combined their inventory and moved to Pueblo Bonito, next to Chaco Canyon.

In 1906 John and Louisa were able to build their own trading post at Oljato, on the Arizona/Utah border in Monument Valley. The 250-mile trek from Pueblo Bonito to Monument Valley was grueling and treacherous. They built their own road for the last ninety miles of the journey, and it took them three weeks to travel what now takes about four hours.

With kind and considerate actions, Louisa earned the trust and friendship of the Paiutes, Utes, and Navajos who visited their remote trading post at Oljato. Eventually they came to her with their quarrels and accepted her resolutions. A Navajo medicine man named Wolfkiller taught Louisa about edible herbs and plants as well as those with medicinal value, and she collected more than three hundred varieties of herbal remedies.

Louisa also became fascinated with Navajo sandpaintings, called "places where the gods come and go" in Navajo. She got Yellow Singer, also known as Sam Chief, to render some of the designs, although not exact copies, in crayon.

The Wetherills opened another trading post in Kayenta in 1910, on the southern edge of Monument Valley. It was there that Louisa hosted a number of scientists, artists, Zane Grey and other authors, and also President Theodore Roosevelt.

In 1944 John Wetherill died after one of his expeditions to the backcountry. Louisa Wetherill died in September 1945. She is considered one of the first Anglos to attempt to understand and preserve Navajo culture and lifestyle, and thought by many Navajos to be one of the greatest friends they ever had.

OPPOSITE: It is no wonder that early twentieth century tourists risked the treacherous two-day ride and hike to magnificent Rainbow Bridge.

drained into the basins and gouged into the Colorado Plateau.

Less than ten million years ago, during the late Tertiary, Navajo Mountain's massive presence created weather systems that helped to increase rainfall and drainage. Now fully developed, the Colorado River system moved vast quantities of gravel, sand, and boulders at powerful speeds to blast away at the sandstone cliffs. At the same time, extended torrential rains known as pluvials drenched the Southwest with rushing water, tearing at canyon walls.

Then during the Pleistocene Epoch, 2.6 million to 11,700 years ago, glaciers moved south over North America. As they expanded, contracted, and melted, the water flow intensified. All of these forces, laccoliths, pluvials, and glaciation, brought about the conditions that formed Rainbow Bridge.

All this time, Bridge Creek's strong flow followed the path of least resistance, cutting deeper and wider trenches, swirling back on itself and forming eddies that cut into the canyon walls. The sandstone walls wore thinner and thinner, turning into hard narrow fins that resisted abrasion. The fin that created Rainbow Bridge rests on Kayenta Sandstone that would not erode. Around five hundred thousand years ago, when the water could no longer cut downward, it began to grind away at both sides of the fin and eventually opened a hole in it. Once it was open, rain, wind, and floods widened the hole from the bottom upward and Bridge Creek shifted its course, flowed through the hole, and formed a trench under what had now become a bridge.

For centuries, the Kayenta Sandstone floor, the powerful creek flow, intense pluvial rains, and wind sculpted the huge space under the bridge. If the Pleistocene climate had not calmed at the end of the last ice age, the structure may have worn away to the

This view of Raplee Ridge is only five miles east of the Goosenecks as the crow flies, but the distance is fourteen miles following the San Juan River's exaggerated twists and turns. TOP: Navajo Mountain dominates the landscape on the Utah/Arizona border twenty miles east of Lake Powell.

Massive geological upheavals millions of years ago resulted in the meandering Goosenecks on the San Juan River near Mexican Hat, Utah.

point where it would have collapsed into the canyon.

The Ancient Puebloans knew this place, and it is considered sacred by the Utes, Paiutes, and Navajos. There are several interpretations for its Navajo name, Nonnezoshe, or Nageelid Nonnezshi, including "rainbow turned to stone" and "the hole in the rock shaped like a rainbow."

Rainbow Bridge's introduction to the rest of the world is yet another example of how explorers are often competitive. Monument Valley's race for the first Anglo to see Rainbow Bridge began in August 1909. The rival leaders were Utah archaeology professor Dr. Byron Cummings and United States General Land Office surveyor William B. Douglass. The two parties combined forces on the last day, but witnesses said Douglass crowded riders off the narrow trail to get to the front of the expedition.

Cummings thought it uncouth to race and began to lead his horse, but the normally subdued guide, John Wetherill, spurred his horse past Douglass and became the first Anglo to stand under the bridge on August 14, 1909. President William Howard Taft declared Rainbow Bridge a national monument three months later. Nowadays you can reach it by boat on Lake Powell or get a Navajo Nation permit and make the long difficult hike. There is no road within miles of Rainbow Bridge.

THE GOOSENECKS

Thirty miles northwest of Goulding's Lodge on the northern edge of Monument Valley, just barely across the Arizona/Utah border and four miles north of Mexican Hat, Utah, Goosenecks State Park offers some cliff-hanging views for adventurous visitors. If you are brave enough, or foolish enough, you can stand on the edge of a cliff with no guardrails or retaining walls overlooking the San Juan River one thousand feet (300 m) below.

Sixty million years ago, the Monument Upwarp formed when blocks of the Earth's crust were pushed up hundreds of feet and the sides of this block of land sloped away from its center. Then the San Juan River, which once looped lazily across a gentle plain, began to cut downward, entrenching itself in this winding path as the surrounding landscape rose slowly around it. These curves called goosenecks produce five winding river miles (8 km) in a straight-line distance of one mile (1.6 km).

Following the path of least resistance between various hardnesses of shale and limestone, the river erodes the outer banks and widens its course while the inner part of the curve flows at a slower pace, depositing sediments on the inside curve, slowing it down and pushing the water to the outer edge of the bend where it erodes even more, creating snaking patterns that geologists call "incised meanders." The second word in

that term comes from the Ancient Greek Maiandros River in present-day Turkey (translated as Maeander in Latin).

LAKE POWELL

There in the vast miles of sand, dust, and wind along the Arizona/Utah border sits an oasis. Lake Powell is a major vacation spot visited by more than two million people every year. It is the second-largest man-made reservoir in the United States by maximum water capacity next to Lake Mead and is named after Civil War Major John Wesley Powell, first to run the Grand Canyon by boat (in 1869).

The water comes from the Colorado River, which starts at the top of the Continental Divide near Estes Park, Colorado, is joined by other major rivers in the Rocky Mountains, merges with the Green River near Moab, Utah, and is stopped by two of the largest reclamation dams in the United States, Glen Canyon and Hoover Dams. It provides water and electric power to seven states in a region that covers an area as large as Spain and Portugal combined. It ends its 1,450-mile (2,333 km) journey just before it reaches the Gulf of California, where the water is diverted and used to produce a large portion of America's vegetables.

By the time the Colorado River reaches Glen Canyon on the Arizona/Utah border, it has joined with the Green River near Moab, Utah, and is large and powerful. It took more than five million years to carve Glen Canyon and the eighty-plus side canyons that merge into it. In the 1960s the 710-foot-high Glen Canyon Dam was constructed to provide irrigation, recreation, and power generation for a vast area reaching hundreds of miles from the dam itself.

The canyons surrounding the lake are some of the most wondrous in the world. Many people have seen stunning pictures of that lone beam of light drilling laser-like straight down into the slot canyon, but not as many know they were taken in Antelope Canyon near Lake Powell. Antelope Canyon is really two canyons with the same name, Upper and Lower. Steep shafts of sunlight are more common in Upper Antelope Canyon, which the Navajos call Tsé bighánílíní, "the place where water runs through rocks." The upper canyon is visited more often because of the flat terrain. The light beam effects occur most often in the summer.

Floods like those that formed these canyons are still a threat. Because of the terrain, there can be little rain in the canyon but torrents several miles away will wash walls of water dangerously through the canyon. National Weather Service alarm horns and elaborate safety systems have reduced the danger and all visitors must be part of a tour led by authorized guides.

The main way to enjoy Lake Powell is on the water, however. At Lake Powell, most houseboats are more like luxury liners than the usual floating RVs of the past. Some of these status-symbol rentals are seventy-five feet long and lavishly equipped with home theater systems, fireplaces, and even hot tubs. And if you would rather someone else take care of the day-to-day details, there are several world-class resorts and marinas right on the lake. While you float serenely on the lake, scenic views change constantly by the mile and by the hour, offering lightshows at sunrise and sunset, with star-filled open skies at night.

Lake Powell is a mecca for all kinds of water sports, including but not limited to power boats, jet skis, waterskiing, swimming, and kayaking. It's also a popular fishing spot, drawing anglers from all over the world.

Canyon X, another phenomenal slot canyon like Antelope Canyon and Secret Canyon near Lake Powell. TOP: Mexican Hat Rock, Mexican Hat, Utah. OPPOSITE: Nothing in this otherworldly sunset picture at Glen Canyon National Recreation Area indicates what decade, century, or millennium we are in. Or for that matter, even what planet we're on. OVERLEAF: Horseshoe Bend, just south of Page, Arizona, is one of the most-photographed features in the Four Corners area, for obvious reasons.

Not only is Lake Powell a great place for tourists and sportsmen, movie producers love it too. In the 1965 epic, *The Greatest Story Ever Told*, director George Stevens said that he decided to shoot in the Southwest instead of the Holy Land because "I wanted to get an effect of grandeur." More than forty movies and television shows have been filmed in and around Lake Powell since then. Looking like something out of this world, the contrast of its blue water with the stark orange-red sandstone shoreline was the perfect choice for *Planet of the Apes* (1968). Its remote setting with no signs of modern life also made it a good location for Westerns: *MacKenna's Gold* (1969), *The Outlaw Josey Wales* (1976), *Wanda Nevada* (1979), *Maverick* (1994), and *Broken Arrow* (1996) were filmed on or around Lake Powell.

And unlike most national parks and recreation areas, this one has a fairly large town almost at the water's edge. Originally called Government Camp, the town of Page was founded in 1957 as a base of operations for the Glen Canyon Dam and was renamed for former Bureau of Reclamation Commissioner John C. Page. The town incorporated in 1975 and is home to the two largest electric power plants in the western United States, a hydroelectric one at the dam and the coal-powered Navajo Generating Station on the east edge of town. Page's new roads and bridge make it the gateway to several national parks, monuments, and Colorado River expeditions.

Just seven miles south of Page is another of those natural wonders for which the Four Corners is famous. Horseshoe

Before the completion of Navajo Bridge in 1929, a ferry was the only way to cross the Colorado River between Arizona and Utah. BELOW: Hundreds of secluded coves make Lake Powell a houseboat haven.

Bend is an incised meander on the Colorado River just as impressive as the Goosenecks on the San Juan River. The overlook at Horseshoe Bend is 1,000 feet (300 m) above the Colorado River. There is a 1.5-mile hiking trail to the edge, and with no guardrails it's quite a thrill to stand at the overlook and look straight down.

GLEN CANYON NATIONAL RECREATION AREA

Created in 1972 for both preservation and recreation purposes, the Glen Canyon National Recreation Area is surrounded by natural wonders and several of the Southwest's most fascinating national parks and monuments.

From Lees Ferry on its southern boundary and Vermilion Cliffs National Monument and Grand Canyon National Park farther southwest, to Grand Staircase-Escalante National Monument on its west flank, and finally Utah's Orange Cliffs and Capitol Reef and Canyonlands National Parks on its northern edge, this recreation area is the hub of what's called the grand circle of Southwestern national parks and monuments.

The Glen Canyon National Recreation Area can be reached from five Lake Powell marinas, and there are houseboat rental facilities, four campgrounds, and two airports inside the perimeter. In addition to hiking trails, there are places set aside for mountain biking, backpacking, and guided tours via boats or four-wheeled vehicles.

MARBLE CANYON

Five miles south of Lees Ferry, the Colorado River flows into Marble Canyon under Navajo Bridge. Considered the highest steel arch bridge in America when it was completed in 1929, it had to be christened with ginger ale instead of the traditional champagne because of Prohibition.

Like many place names all over the world, the name of this canyon is misleading. There is no marble in Marble Canyon. Major John Wesley Powell, a geology professor at Illinois Wesleyan University at the time of the expedition, knew it was not marble. But he said, "The limestone of the canyon is often polished, and it makes a beautiful marble. Sometimes the rocks are of many colors—white, gray, pink, and purple, with saffron tints."

The Navajo Bridge is one of only seven land crossings for 750 miles along the Colorado River and it rises 467 feet above the river. A new, similar bridge opened in 1995 and the old one remains as a pedestrian bridge, offering excellent sunset views of the Colorado River, the surrounding cliffs, and the rare California condors who like to roost under the bridge.

VERMILION CLIFFS NATIONAL MONUMENT

Most of Vermilion Cliffs National Monument is a flat, sandy, isolated plateau. It covers 294,000 acres of remote uninhabited country in the Four Corners. There are a few outcroppings of multicolored swirling sandstone formations, but the monument is named for its main attraction. The Vermilion Cliffs themselves are said to be one of the most spectacular, continuous, expansive cliff faces in the United States. Named for

There is no marble in Marble Canyon, but the weather-polished limestone walls resemble it.

their scarlet red variegated Chinle Formation sandstone, the cliffs are thirty miles long and up to two thousand feet high in some places.

The U.S. Fish and Wildlife Service operates one of its three California Condor Recovery Program breeding and release sites at Vermilion Cliffs. This endangered species is the largest flying land bird in North America. They have a wingspan of 9.5 feet (2.9 m), can weigh up to 25 pounds as adults, and can soar and glide up to 50 miles per hour and travel 100 miles or more per day, which explains why many are seen under the Navajo bridge 30 miles away from their home. By the late 1930s, condors were found only in California, and by 1982, the total population worldwide was just twenty-two birds. The reintroduction of captive-bred condors began in 1992 in California, and they started the second program in Arizona in 1996 with ten condors. By 2005 the total number of condors had increased to 270, and in December 2016, U.S. Fish and Wildlife Service reported a world total condor population of 446, with 276 of those living in the wild.

 ## 3. The Northwest Quadrant

FREMONT CULTURE

This prehistoric culture got its name because the first archaeological sites for this culture were discovered along the Fremont River. These hunter-gatherers lived in natural rock shelters and pit houses in Idaho, Nevada, Utah, and Colorado between 600 and 1300 CE. They were loosely organized bands of families and had to be flexible and adaptable to changes in their surroundings.

Fremont people probably never numbered more than 10,000 and lived varied lifestyles. Some were settled farmers, others were nomadic hunter-gatherers, and other groups shifted between these two lifestyles. They hunted and trapped large and small game and fish, using snares, nets, fishhooks, bows and arrows, and atlatls. The Fremont Culture gathered edible nuts, berries, and shrubs and grew corn, beans, and squash along the river bottoms.

Although they differed in many things, Fremont Culture regional subgroups from Elko, Nevada, to Pocatello, Idaho, to Grand Junction, Colorado, and St. George, Utah, all made baskets and moccasins in a particular style, as well as clay figurines and distinctive thin-walled gray pottery. They did not live in cities or build multistoried dwellings like their Ancestral Puebloan neighbors to the south, however.

Fremont rock art depicts deer, lizards, bison, bighorn sheep, abstract designs, and handprints. TOP: This curious formation is in the White Pocket section of Vermilion Cliffs National Monument.

Larger Fremont settlements dwindled between 1300 and 1500 CE. As with the other peoples, drought sent them away from big villages and back to semi-nomadic foraging. About a thousand years ago, the hunter-gatherer ancestors of the Ute, Paiute, and Shoshone peoples may have migrated into the area.

GRAND STAIRCASE-ESCALANTE NATIONAL MONUMENT

Grand Staircase-Escalante National Monument is bordered by Glen Canyon National Recreation Area on the east, Grand Canyon National Park on the south, Bryce Canyon National Park on the west, and Capitol Reef on the northeast, and there are also several state parks, a national forest, and a primitive area in the region. The Grand Staircase-Escalante National Monument area was the last place in the United States to be mapped, and not many tourists visit its beautiful rock formations because of its lack of roads. Signing an executive order on December 4, 2017, President Donald Trump reduced this monument by nearly 47 percent.

The area is divided into three geographical sections whose rock formations span more than two hundred million years of Earth's history from the Permian to Cretaceous eras. The westernmost third, Grand Staircase, got its name because of its series of broad rock benches, terraces, plateaus, and cliffs.

The Cockscomb, a series of hogbacks (long narrow ridges with narrow crests and steep slopes on both sides) separates the Grand Staircase from the Kaiparowits Basin, a series of Cretaceous-era plateaus, buttes, and mesas. On its eastern edge, the Straight Cliffs mark the basin's eastern boundary with the Escalante Canyons.

This area is named for Spanish explorer and priest, Father Silvestre Veléz de Escalante, assistant to Father Atanasio Domínguez in a 1776–1777 exploration to develop a route from Santa Fe, New Mexico, to Monterey, California. Plagued by dehydration and disease, the group reached the Cedar City,

It's a long journey by dirt road and then hiking to reach Golden Cathedral in Neon Canyon, Grand Staircase-Escalante National Monument, but well worth the effort. LEFT: On Yellow Rock, in Grand Staircase, rock formations resemble thousands of stone steps rising hundreds of feet.

Utah, area on October 11, 1776, and turned back. Their return route went through what is now called Escalante Canyons. Here, the Escalante River scoured out a maze of towering walls and left stunning grottoes in hidden canyon bottoms.

More late-Cretaceous terrestrial fossils have been found in Grand Staircase-Escalante Monument than anywhere else in the United States. Twenty new dinosaur species have been discovered since 2000, capturing the remains of an ancient tropical rainforest and providing a 30-million-year record of prehistoric species from mosses and ferns to giant dinosaurs.

Inhabited by humans since the Clovis Culture moved in 13,000 years ago, both Ancestral Pueblo and Fremont Culture people lived in this area from 950 to 1100 CE. Around 1100 CE they formed a blend of Ancestral Pueblo and Fremont cultures. In the mid-1200s, the farmers moved south and the Southern Paiute hunter-gatherers moved in, although there was also cultural blending and intermarriage. Euro-American pioneers began farming and ranching in the monument in the 1850s but many communities were abandoned because of the harsh climate.

NATURAL BRIDGES
NATIONAL MONUMENT

"A lot of rocks, a lot of sand, more rocks, more sand, and wind enough to blow it away."

—FEDERAL WRITERS' PROJECT,
WPA Guide to Utah, the Beehive State, 1941

Natural Bridges National Monument is an area of spectacu-lar rock formations, including three immense water-carved bridges that give the monument its name. The monument is forty-six miles west of Blanding, Utah, and 121 miles from Four Corners National Monument. Until the 1950s, there were no paved roads, and visitors who wanted to visit Kachina and Sipapu Bridges had to get there on horseback.

From seventy-five to fifty million years ago, the Laramide orogeny raised Triassic and Permian ocean beds up a thousand feet in slightly tilted plateaus where river drainage and rainwa-ter carved out caves, arches, and natural bridges. As layers of rock were pushed upward, the relatively newer layers eroded faster, laying bare the white quartz sand of the older Cedar Mesa Sandstone.

Nature worked the same process here as described for Rainbow Bridge. Fast-running, meandering water cut down through layers of sandstone and then holed through tall, nar-row, softer sandstone fins with harder top layers to create natu-ral bridges. Natural bridges are rare geological features, but to have three of the largest ones in North America form so close to each other that you can hike from one to another is unique.

Government surveyor William Douglass gave the bridges Hopi names in honor of their ancestors, the Ancestral Puebloans, who lived there between 2000 BCE and 500 CE. Dancing figure petroglyphs at the base of one bridge caused Douglass to name it Kachina after the Hopi dancing spirits. Sipapu is the hole in the earth where an older world opens into the new one. The third bridge's name, Owachomo, means "rock mound" and is named after a rock formation on top of the east end of the bridge.

Kachina is the most recently formed bridge, estimated as ten million years old. It has a relatively small opening with a thick and bulky overhead span. It is 210 feet (64 m) tall, 204 feet (62 m) across, 44 feet (13 m) wide and 93 feet (28 m) thick.

Sipapu Bridge is the largest and considered most spectacu-lar of the three. It is older, as shown by its larger opening and thinner span. It is 220 feet (67 m) tall, 268 feet (82 m) across, 31 feet (9.5 m) wide, and 53 feet (16 m) thick. While weath-ering continues to enlarge the opening, the base of Sipapu is now 167 feet above the streambed, so there should be no more stream erosion.

Owachomo is the oldest, thinnest, and smallest of the bridges and its span has worn away to just 9 feet (3 m) thick at its thinnest point. Its height is 106 feet (32 m), span is 180 feet (55 m), and it is 27 feet (8 m) wide. The most fragile and elegant of the three spans, it may collapse within the next few centuries.

Horse Collar Ruin, named for its doorways wider at the top like a horse collar, is the fourth main attraction at Natural Bridges National Monument. The site's extreme isolation

Sipapu Bridge, Natural Bridges National Monument.

OPPOSITE: Long Canyon, Grand Staircase-Escalante National Monument.

43

before the middle of the twentieth century accounts for its well-preserved condition, including a kiva with original centuries-old roof and interior.

The Archaic people, 7000 BCE to 500 CE, were the first to occupy the area, followed by Ancestral Puebloans and finally Paiutes and Navajos arrived. A 1904 article in *National Geographic* gave the bridges international attention, and President Theodore Roosevelt declared the area a national monument in 1908.

BEARS EARS NATIONAL MONUMENT

Just north of Natural Bridges, one of the earliest national monuments to be created by executive order, you will find Bears Ears National Monument, one of the most recent ones. Established by President Barack Obama on December 28, 2016, Bears Ears National Monument's size was cut 85 percent by President Donald Trump on December 4, 2017.

The monument protects public lands surrounding a pair of sandstone mesas called Bears Ears and a rock-climbing corridor called Indian Creek. The monument is co-managed by the United States Forest Service, the Bureau of Land Management, and five Native American tribes: Hopi, Navajo Nation, Pueblo of Zuni, Ute Indian Tribe of the Uintah and Ouray Reservation, and the Ute Mountain Ute, all of which have ancestral links to the region. There are more than one hundred thousand archaeological sites in the monument dating to 13,000 BCE.

CAPITOL REEF NATIONAL PARK

Aerial photography of Waterpocket Fold in Capitol Reef National Park helps capture the Four Corners' grand scale. LEFT: The Butler Wash cliff dwelling in the Bears Ears National Monument area was built by Ancestral Puebloans about 1200 CE.

Like Natural Bridges National Monument, Capitol Reef National Park's geology also dates from 50 to 70 million years ago as a result of the Laramide orogeny. It created a 100-mile-long warp in the Earth's crust called Waterpocket Fold, a rocky monocline of layered sandstone steps, some lifted more than 7,000 feet (2,134 m) from their ocean-bed surface. Then the whole Colorado Plateau lifted up 15 to 20 million years ago and erosion exposed numerous arches, cliffs, domes, pinnacles, and monoliths.

Starting as a national monument in 1937 and changed to national park status in 1971, the park is 60 miles (97 km) long from north to south but only about 6 miles (9.7 km) wide in some places. It is named for Capitol Reef, the most impressive feature. At that location, ten thousand feet of monumental red sandstone sedimentary cliffs tower above the Fremont River, and its white Navajo Sandstone domes resemble the architectural domes of many capitol buildings throughout the United States. The second word in its name is for its barrier-like cliffs similar to oceanic coral reefs. The park's formations range from Permian to Cretaceous eras (270 to 80 million years old).

Near the northwestern edge of the park, Cathedral Valley is another main attraction with freestanding reddish-orange Entrada Sandstone cliffs. In the same area, flowing and dissolving gypsum created Glass Mountain, a fifteen-foot-high mound of large selenite crystals.

Over thousands of years, Capitol Reef National Park has been inhabited by archaic hunter-gatherers, Fremont culture

Sunset on the scenic drive, Capitol Reef National Park, Utah.
TOP: Temple of the Moon (left) and Temple of the Sun, Capitol
Reef National Park.

TRAIL OF THE ANCIENTS
SCENIC BYWAY

The Four Corners area has so many things to see that a
federally designated national scenic byway was created to
link a number of the main attractions together in a network of highways traveling from the Four Corners Monument to Monument Valley; Valley of the Gods; Gooseneck
State Park; Bluff, Utah; Edge of the Cedars State Park in
Blanding, Utah; Butler Wash and Mule Canyon Ruins between Blanding and Natural Bridges National Monument;
the Grand Gulch Primitive Area south of Natural Bridges;
Three Kiva Pueblo; and Hovenweep National Monument.

Edge of the Cedars Pueblo, Edge of the Cedars State Park
Museum, Utah.

farmers, and finally Mormon pioneers, who said they created
almost a Garden of Eden in Wayne County, Utah. Currently
the heart of Capitol Reef National Park's administrative center,
the former town of Fruita is located in south-central Utah at
the confluence of the Fremont River and Sulphur Creek.

Mormons led by Nels Johnson settled it in the 1870s. They
called the place Junction, and the name Fruita came into being
around 1902 because of its abundant apple, pear, and peach
orchards.

UTES, SHOSHONES, BANNOCKS, GOSHUTES, AND PAIUTES

The Utes call themselves Noochew, Nuutsiu, or Nuciu, which means "The People." When the Spanish encountered these Native Americans in the late sixteenth century, they called them Yutah, which translates as "people who live in the 'high land,' or 'land of the sun.'" Their language group is Shoshonean (or Numic), a subgroup of Uto-Aztecan, the major language group of the majority of western Native Americans.

The Shoshone and Bannock tribes live in northwest Utah, the Utes and Goshutes live in central and southeast Utah, and the Southern Paiutes live in west central and southwest Utah. According to Ute traditions, Sinawav created the Utes and placed them in the mountains of Utah and Colorado where they still live today. They have always been there and will always be there.

However, anthropologists indicate that up to twelve bands of twenty to one hundred each left western Canada and Alaska in the thirteenth century to inhabit Utah and may have driven other cultures into Arizona and northwest New Mexico. The Utes encountered conflicts with many other Indian cultures, including Apache, Cheyenne, Comanche, Hopi, Navajo, and Paiute. Ute hunting trails through the vast deserts and rugged mountains became invaluable to the Spanish and Euro-American settlers who moved into the area from the 1600s through the 1800s.

The Utes never had an encompassing tribal organization; like Apaches they had hunting and raiding expedition leaders and spiritual heads with no overall chief. They followed semi-nomadic seasonal routes, hunting and harvesting plants. Utes lived in brush wickiups and under ramadas in southern and western areas and in rawhide teepees in their eastern territories.

Ute lifestyle and culture changed abruptly when they acquired horses from the Spanish. Horses allowed them to hunt buffalo over seventy-nine million acres of the Great Basin area and parts of Wyoming, Colorado, Utah, Arizona, and New Mexico as they adopted the Plains Culture traditions of raiding and trading.

American fur trappers entered what is now the state of Utah in the early 1800s, and Mormon settlers arrived in 1847. Trouble began when farmers moved in and wanted the Utes to settle in one place. Crop failures showed the Indians that their traditional roaming, hunter-gatherer, raiding-and-trading lifestyle was the only way to avoid starvation. President Abraham Lincoln set aside the two-million-acre Uintah Valley Reservation in 1861, but a Ute war leader named Autenquer (Black Hawk) roused Southern Paiutes and Utes, and their resistance was known as the Black Hawk War (1863–1868), which ended in defeat for the Native Americans. Peaceful Ute leader Tabby-To-Kwanah led the Utes and Paiutes onto the reservation in 1869. U.S. Government officials moved the Yamparka and

This photograph of five Ute women was taken around 1899.

Rose and Hopkins/Library of Congress

Parianuc Utes to the Uintah Reservation in 1881 and the peaceful Taviwac (also known as Uncompahgre) Utes to the Ouray Reservation, another two-million-acre settlement adjoining the Uintah location.

Conflicts flared between the various bands and even more trouble arose in 1887 with the passage of the Dawes Severalty Act. This federal law abandoned the reservation system in many places, gave land parcels of 160 acres to individual Indian families, and opened the rest of the land to white settlement. The allotment and open land were often intermingled, often described as checkerboard areas at the time. Congress repealed the Dawes Act in 1934 and replaced it with the Indian Reorganization Act, but it did not alter the fact that ninety million acres had been removed from Indian ownership throughout the United States.

Confusing as it might be, there are towns in both Utah and Colorado, plus a county in Colorado, all named Ouray. In the 1880s, historian Hubert Howe Bancroft described the town of Ouray, Colorado: "It is named after the Ute chief, for whose friendship the white people were grateful, at a time when his word might have precipitated war." Chief Ouray was born in Taos, New Mexico, and worked as a shepherd on Mexican ranches. At age eighteen he moved to Colorado and soon became a leader and spokesman because he spoke several languages and had lived in more than one culture. Known as a dangerous and cunning warrior in his youth, his attitudes shifted when he realized that white settlement could not be halted.

In a recent count, approximately 1,500 Utes still spoke their native language and they are creating an alphabet so that it can be written down. They now teach preschoolers to become fluent in the language, and the elders pass on their folklore. One of the stories they tell is about Sleeping Ute Mountain, which when viewed from the side looks like a reclining Indian with his headdress pointing north. He was once a great warrior god who became wounded and fell into a deep sleep. Blood from his wound turned into water and rain clouds fell from his pockets. He is covered with a blanket that changes colors with the seasons.

Today there are three main groups of Ute people. The largest is the Northern Ute, then the Southern Ute, and the Ute Mountain Ute. Most of them live on one of the three reservations, Uintah-Ouray (3,500 members), Southern Ute (1,500), and Ute Mountain (2,000 members). The latter is situated primarily in Colorado but extends into New Mexico and Utah as well.

BLUFF, BLANDING, AND MONTICELLO

"There is, in the country, a vivid eternal peace, vastness, and power."
—**FEDERAL WRITERS' PROJECT**,
WPA Guide to Utah, the Beehive State, 1941

Just thirty miles from the spot where four states meet, you'll see an unusual welcome sign as you reach the edge of Bluff, Utah. It's a massive slab of peach-colored sandstone on a red concrete base and in big black letters the sign says, "Welcome to Bluff, established 650 CE." Bluff residents appreciate their "deep history," whether it's geological, archaeological, or pioneer settlement. Bluff is a leading spot for adventurers to put in their boats and kayaks to ride the San Juan River rapids. The longer trips end at Clay Hills Boat Ramp on Lake Powell, after sixty miles of twists, turns, and rapids.

Ancient peoples hunted mammoths here 11,000 years ago, and their hunter-gatherer lifestyle gave way to corn-based agriculture and pit house construction around 600 CE. Around 800 CE they built a great kiva at the base of Twin Rocks on the east side of what is now modern Bluff. In the centuries that followed, they constructed great houses, great kivas, and roads similar to those created in Chaco Canyon, New Mexico, at that time. Bluff's main archaeological attraction, the multistory stone masonry Bluff Great House, was part of this expansion and remained in use for two hundred years.

The sites around Bluff were abandoned around 1250 CE and the people moved south to Arizona and northwestern New Mexico. By the late 1500s, seminomadic bands of Navajos, Paiutes, and Utes hunted rabbits, deer, and mountain sheep and irrigated corn, beans, and squash around what is now Bluff, Utah.

In 1880, Mormon pioneers founded Bluff, the first Anglo settlement in the San Juan River area of southeast Utah. Seventy families, a total of 250 people, took six months to travel 260 miles under grueling winter conditions to get to Bluff. At one point the men spent six weeks blasting an opening in a 1,200-foot cliff known after that as "Hole in the Rock," that can still be seen at buoy 66 on Lake Powell or by following the primitive Hole in the Rock Trail that runs southwest from the town of Escalante, Utah. Although they had intended to settle on Montezuma Creek, the exhausted pioneers reached a flat spot along the river twenty miles short of their goal. The San Juan River valley looked like good farmland, so they called it Bluff City after the towering sandstone bluffs.

When flooding made farming difficult, residents raised stock. They built stately Victorian-style homes of cut sandstone

The Procession Panel on the eastern side of Comb Ridge was also created by the Ancestral Puebloans.

TOP: Pueblo I style Black/Red pitcher with dog effigy, from the Edge of the Cedars Museum, Blanding, Utah.

block during the cattle boom of 1886–1905. They could never tame the San Juan River, however, and many pioneer families left Bluff for Grayson, a town twenty-three miles north on U.S. Highway 191. But you can't go to Grayson anymore; it is now known as Blanding, Utah.

Why would a town change its name? Blanding was originally named Grayson after pioneer Nellie Grayson Lyman. Then a businessman named Thomas W. Bicknell made Grayson citizens an offer they couldn't refuse. In 1914, Bicknell offered any town in Utah a 1,000-book library to change their name to his. But if Bicknell gave them the books, why did Grayson change its name to Blanding? Two towns answered his request, and Bicknell, Utah, another town 181 miles northwest of Blanding, tied for the honor. So each town got five hundred books. Blanding was named for Bicknell's wife's maiden name, Amelia Blanding.

Mormons Walter C. Lyman and Joseph Lyman and their families founded Blanding in 1897. Ancestral Puebloans lived in the area on White Mesa near Blue Mountain as early as 600 CE because of local springs and pools. Later the Utes, Navajos, and Spaniards also frequented the area because of its water supply. Today the economy hinges on mineral processing, agriculture, tourism, and transportation.

Blanding is the gateway to many natural and archaeological sites in southeastern Utah. In addition to those mentioned earlier in this book, it is on the edge of Cedar Mesa archaeological and wilderness area. That mesa reaches ninety miles from the southern Utah border to Capitol Reef National Park and covers nearly four hundred square miles (1,036 sq km) of land.

On the northwest edge of Blanding, Utah, Edge of the Cedars State Park Museum has to be the most accessible Ancestral Pueblo ruins anywhere in the Four Corners region. It's less than a mile and a half (2.42 km) from the center of town, and you could walk to it from most of the town's lodging places. In addition to the partially restored dwelling site inhabited from 700 to 1220 CE, the park has an archaeological site, museum, and research center, and it serves as a regional archaeological repository.

If you start at Bluff (elevation 4,324 feet/1,318 m) and go up twenty-five miles north on U.S. Highway 191, you'll reach Blanding (elevation 6,106 feet/1,861 m). If you keep climbing another thousand feet in the next twenty miles north, you will reach the town of Monticello, Utah (elevation 7,070 feet/2,154 m). The towns are close enough that you might call them three sisters. If you happen to have three sisters as this author does, you know that while they are often close, they can also be very different. Monticello is the sister who stands out among the three. Rather than sitting on a flat mesa, the town rests at the base of the Abajo Mountains. Known locally as the Blue Mountains, they are a small range west of town in the Manti-La Sal National Forest. Often snow-capped Abajo Peak looms over Monticello at 11,360 feet (3,463 m).

MOAB, UTAH

Fifty miles north of Monticello is Moab, the center of the largest number of tourist attractions in the Four Corners. The Colorado River bends around Moab, so it is about a mile to the north of the town and also a mile and a half to its west. With Canyonlands National Park and Dead Horse Point State Park to its west and Arches National Park to the north, Moab serves as a base camp for boating, kayaking, mountain biking, and rafting. A city full of attractions and accommodations, Moab is the closest to the most fantastic arches, spires, and canyons.

Mormons named their settlement Moab, the Biblical land beyond the Jordan River. Spanish explorer Juan de Rivera found this to be a good crossing place in 1765, but it was sixty-five years later before Europeans returned, when Mexican soldiers blazed a trail between Santa Fe, New Mexico, and Los Angeles, California. Pathfinder John C. Fremont dubbed it "The Old Spanish Trail." When connected with the Santa Fe Trail, it created the final arduous link for the first transcontinental route from America's east coast to its west coast. Uranium mining was big business in the area in the 1950s, but today the intersections are jammed with tour vans, boats on trailers, and four-wheeled vehicles with mountain bikes strapped to their roofs.

The Titan, an astounding 900-feet-tall (274 meters) sandstone spire is part of Fisher Towers near Moab.

CANYONLANDS NATIONAL PARK

*"The most weird, wonderful, magical place on earth—
there is nothing else like it anywhere."*

> —EDWARD ABBEY, *Postcards from Ed: Dispatches
> and Salvos from an American Iconoclast*, 2006.

If southern Utah were a three-ring circus, Canyonlands National Park would be in the center ring under the big top with Arches National Park and Deadhorse State Park as the sideshows. In Canyonlands, the Green River and the Colorado River join to form the largest river in the West. The two great rivers cut deep rugged canyons into the park's 340,000 acres (1,375 sq km) full of massive sandstone arches, mesas, and spires.

The park is divided into four distinct districts: the Needles, the Maze, the Island in the Sky, and the two rivers themselves. Island in the Sky is situated on top of sandstone cliffs 2,000 feet (600 m) above the rivers just upstream from where they join. There is a paved road along the top of the promontory with several pullouts that provide excellent bird's-eye views of Canyonlands' rivers and canyons.

Not only are there fantastic views but Canyonlands is also a popular destination for hikers, mountain bikers, backpackers, four-wheelers, and kayakers. For more than ten years, an average of 400,000 visitors reach Canyonlands per year, and in 2016 that number increased to 776,218 visitors who came to experience one of the most impressive sections of the Colorado Plateau.

Canyonland National Park's Great Gallery in Horseshoe Canyon features some of the most significant rock art in North America. The images date from 2000 BCE to as recent as 1300 CE. TOP: It is not clear who built this stone circle in Canyonlands National Park or whether it was used as a kiva-style ceremonial structure. OVERLEAF: Sunrise at Mesa Arch, Canyonlands National Park.

NEWSPAPER ROCK
STATE HISTORIC MONUMENT

This state monument has just one feature: a 200-square-foot Wingate sandstone rock covered so thickly with hundreds of ancient Indian petroglyphs (rock carvings) that it reminds one of a newspaper. The pictures were pecked into the dark "desert varnish," the brown, black, or maroon-tinged manganese deposits coating the sandstone and caused by rain and bacteria. This rock is one of the best-preserved and largest collections of rock carvings in the Southwest, featuring a wide variety of human, animal, and abstract forms.

The Navajo call it Tsé Hone (a rock that tells a story) and archaeologists believe that the first pictures were carved more than two thousand years ago. Rock art is also visible on nearby cliffs, but Newspaper Rock is the main attraction.

Newspaper Rock features more petroglyphs per square inch than any other location.

DEAD HORSE POINT STATE PARK

Along with Horseshoe Bend and the Goosenecks, Dead Horse Point is one of the most photogenic gooseneck incised meanders on the Colorado Plateau. Looming 2,000 feet above the Colorado River, these steep cliffs carved by wind and water furnish a most phenomenal view that is difficult to portray with photographs, let alone words. The scale and scope have to be experienced in person to get the full impact.

ARCHES NATIONAL PARK

This 119-square-mile (310 sq km) national park has more than 2,000 arches in various blends of red, orange, and pink sandstone, making it the highest density of arches anywhere in the world.

Arches differ from natural bridges in the way that nature creates them. Natural bridges occur only where floodwaters run strong and fast in deep channels, while arches are formed by gravity, wind, and rain removing sandstone particles gradually to achieve the same "holing-through" effect. While arches can develop in many kinds of rock, sandstone's combination of being strong enough to support tall cliffs and yet soft and porous enough to erode easily make it a prime material for arch formation.

New arches are still being formed, and old ones collapse. Delicate Arch is the star of the show, but Balanced Rock, Double Arch, Frame Arch, and Landscape Arch are also photographers' favorites. Delicate Arch is 65 feet (20 m) tall and is considered the most impressive formation in the park. When the Winter Olympic Games were held in Salt Lake City

Kokopelli petroglyphs, Puerco Pueblo, Petrified Forest, Arizona.

KOKOPELLI

Of all the ancient figures pecked and painted onto the sandstone cliffs and pottery throughout the Southwest, Kokopelli is the leading celebrity. His simple stick figure drawn in profile began to appear around 1000 CE in the Four Corners area and spread through all parts of each of the four states over four centuries. Fewer and fewer images appeared after that, and by the time the Spaniards arrived in the mid-1500s, there were no more new images of Kokopelli.

Depending on the area and the legend, Kokopelli was a hunter, minstrel, trader, storyteller, trickster, a seducer of maidens, or any combination of those traits. The Hopi katsina Kokopölö is portrayed with a hump and brings rain, good crops, and human fertility. The Zuni katsina Paiyatemu, the flute-playing cicada, plays to bring the rainy season. Regional Native American artists still use his figure for baskets, silverwork, textiles, and other art forms.

Sunset at Dead Horse Point State Park. BELOW: North Window Arch frames Turret Arch, Arches National Park.

OVERLEAF: Balanced Rock is one of Arches National Park's major attractions.

in 2002, the Olympic Torch was carried under the arch on the way to the games, and legislators made it the official emblem printed on Utah automobile license plates. The area became a national monument in 1929 and was redesignated as a national park in 1971.

 ## 4. The Northeast Quadrant

McINNIS CANYONS NATIONAL CONSERVATION AREA AND COLORADO NATIONAL MONUMENT

One of the best things about the Four Corners is the amount of land that has been set aside for nature and wildlife preservation. As soon as you cross from Utah to Colorado on Interstate 70, you have entered the McInnis Canyons National Conservation Area. Named after Congressman Scott McInnis, the area conserves 123,400 acres (499 sq km) of sandstone canyons, arches, and spires around a twenty-four-mile stretch of the Colorado River. Its status allows hiking, biking, non-motorized boating, and many other activities. Within the area, Rattlesnake Arches features the highest concentration of natural arches in Colorado and is second only to Arches National Park for the most in the world. Unlike Arches, there is no motorized vehicle access.

However, adjacent to the east is Colorado National Monument—same geology, much easier access. The monument's Rim Rock Drive offers spectacular views into steep-walled canyons on the east edge of the Colorado Plateau's mesa lands. The monument covers 32 square miles (82 sq km). There are more than forty hiking trails through red rock canyons as beautiful as Sedona, Arizona, without the crowds.

GRAND JUNCTION, COLORADO

What's so Grand about Grand Junction? It's where the Gunnison and Grand Rivers meet, of course, so that explains the "Junction" part. But what about that first word in the name? *There is no Grand River anymore.* In 1921, after thirteen years of political effort, U.S. Representative Edward T. Taylor convinced the Committee on Interstate and Foreign Commerce to pass a resolution on to Congress to change the Grand River's name to the Colorado River. Until that time, the stretch of what we now call the Colorado River that ran from its source near Estes Park, Colorado, down to Utah was called the Grand River. At that time it only became the Colorado River when it joined the Green River near Moab. Hence, the names Grand Lake and Grand Junction.

Because of its location on a major freeway and those two rivers, Grand Junction is the largest city on the Rocky Mountains' western slope. This is also the heart of Colorado's wine country. With an elevation of 4,700 feet (1,432 m), the twenty-five mile stretch from Palisade to Fruita, Colorado, along Interstate 70 boasts more than twenty vineyards and wineries. It is a relatively arid land with frequent sunshine and mild winters, just the right ingredients for grape growing.

Paleo Indians lived here as early as 11,000 BCE, and then Archaic Indians began rudimentary farming. The Fremont Culture then lived there in caves, rock shelters, and pit houses from 700 to 1200 CE. The Ute tribe replaced them, as noted earlier.

The Painted Wall, Gunnison River, Black Canyon of the Gunnison National Park, Colorado. TOP: Colorado National Monument is lesser known than other canyons in the Four Corners area but just as impressive. OPPOSITE: Delicate Arch, the most famous in Arches National Park, is featured on the Utah state license plate.

SILVERTON AND DURANGO, COLORADO

Silverton, Colorado, has a billboard on the edge of town in old-time lettering that says, "Welcome to Silverton, a Victorian Mining Town." It was founded in 1874 after prospectors found a rich silver vein in the San Juan Mountains. They found gold in 1882 and the mines continued to close and reopen through floods and even the 1929 stock market crash, continuing operations as recently as 2015.

Nestled at an elevation of 9,318 feet (2,836 m) above sea level and flanked by the San Juan and Rio Grande National Forests, the 1.86 million-acre (7,530 sq km) region includes the San Luis Valley, the world's largest agricultural alpine valley. In addition to harvesting lettuce and potatoes, they are the main barley supplier for the Coors Brewing Company.

Silverton is a Rocky Mountain/Continental Divide town unlike Utah's Colorado Plateau towns sitting atop hot dry sandstone mesas. The Continental Divide runs atop a series of mountain crests from Canada to Central America. When rain and snow hit these high peaks, water either runs down their western slopes to the Pacific Ocean or their eastern slopes to the Atlantic Ocean. The Continental Divide zigzags roughly ten miles east of Silverton and then ten miles south of it.

Most people have probably never heard of this small alpine town before and those who do know it are likely fans of the Durango and Silverton Narrow Gauge Railroad. The Denver & Rio Grande Railway founded the town of Durango, Colorado, in 1880 and their train began hauling passengers and freight from Durango to Silverton by 1882. Constructed primarily to haul gold and silver ore out of the San Juan Mountains, it is estimated that at least three hundred million dollars in valuable metals have been carried on this train.

The famous narrow gauge track out of Silverton was completed in 1887. The train suffered many challenges, from floods to economic downturns to the 1918 Spanish Influenza Pandemic, but continued to operate. In 1947 the owners threatened to shut it down for lack of profits, but the staff persevered, promoted tourism, and kept the line alive. Hollywood saved the day by filming at least five major motion pictures

Constructed in 1908, the San Juan County Courthouse (left) is part of a federally designated National Historic Landmark District. LEFT: The Durango & Silverton Railway locomotive leaving Silverton, Colorado. OPPOSITE: Ice Lake, Fuller Peak, Vermilion Peak, and Golden Horn near Silverton, Colorado. OVERLEAF: A gondola near Telluride, Colorado, provides a completely different perspective of the Four Corners area.

that showcased the train: *Across the Wide Missouri, Around the World in 80 Days, Denver & Rio Grande, Ticket to Tomahawk,* and *Viva Zapata!* all premiered in the 1950s, and the train became famous all over again with the epic blockbuster western *Butch Cassidy and the Sundance Kid* in 1969. The Durango & Silverton continues with year-round train service using 100 percent coal-burning steam engines.

Fifty miles south of Silverton and three thousand feet downhill, Durango, Colorado, sits on the banks of the Animas River in the San Juan Mountains. Founded by railroad administrators and named after Durango, Mexico, its abundant water and favorable terrain and climate made it a stopping point on the Old Spanish Trail in the eighteenth century. Going back even farther to the first people to arrive in North America, the Clovis Culture hunters lived there as early as 12,000 BCE. Durango is a popular fly-fishing site and a favorite spot for kayaking, hiking, and rock climbing. The railroad is one of its major attractions, but it is also the gateway to Mesa Verde National Park.

MESA VERDE NATIONAL PARK

In Mesa Verde National Park, forty miles east of Durango, Colorado, you will encounter the most exceptional prehistoric cliff dwelling sites, more than five thousand in all. This 50,000-acre park (202 sq km) includes six hundred cliff dwellings, and receives more than half a million visitors per year. Because of its exceptional archaeological presence, the United Nations Educational, Scientific and Cultural Organization (UNESCO) declared Mesa Verde National Park a World Heritage Site in 1978.

Mesa Verde means "green table" in Spanish and is so named because it sits on top of a verdant mesa at 8,500 feet (2,590 m) above sea level. The Ancestral Puebloans built pit houses here around 550 CE because there were natural springs in the area and water runoff at the bottom of the cliffs. Like the Hopi mesas, there is almost no water on top of the mesa.

For the next five hundred years they built underground ceremonial kivas and multistoried apartment structures known as pueblos. After 1200 CE they moved from the top of the mesa and into the large alcoves under the sandstone cliff overhangs. Some Mesa Verde cliff dwellings seem to defy gravity and others blend perfectly with their surroundings. While most had fewer than ten rooms, Cliff Palace had more than 150 rooms and 20 kivas. Drought and other circumstances caused the Ancestral Puebloans to vacate the area around 1300 CE. Their descendants probably migrated south and southwest to the Rio Grande area around Albuquerque, Santa Fe, and Taos, as well as the Hopi mesas in Arizona.

The area is in such a remote and formidable location that no one reached the ruins until Richard Wetherill and his brother-in-law Charles Mason stumbled onto them in 1888 while looking for stray cattle. Richard was the brother of John Wetherill, Monument Valley trading post owner. Richard had been searching for ruins in southwest Colorado when a Ute Indian named Acowitz supposedly told him of a canyon where there were many Ancient Ones' houses.

Ancestral Puebloans built with wood beams and sandstone blocks. The blocks were cemented together with mortar made of soil, water, and ash. LEFT: Since bowls like this one from Mesa Verde National Park were rarely blackened by fire, archaeologists deduce that they were used for mixing or serving food and not cooking it. TOP: One of the larger dwellings at Mesa Verde National Park, Cliff Palace was inhabited from 1190 CE to 1300 CE. It has 23 kivas and 150 rooms.

CORTEZ AND DOLORES, COLORADO — CENTER OF THE ANCIENT WORLD

CANYONS OF THE ANCIENTS NATIONAL MONUMENT

While the ruins at Canyons of the Ancients are not as impressive architecturally as those at Mesa Verde, they far surpass it in number of sites. This 176,000-acre monument (712 sq km) has the highest density of archaeological sites in the United States. The total number of archaeological sites, including those not fully recorded, is estimated at 30,000.

The earliest sites at this location date from the Developmental Pueblo period, 750 to 1100 BCE, and habitation ends during the Great Pueblo period, 1100 to 1300 CE. While almost all other Ancient Pueblo dwellers left their large communities around 1350 CE, those at Canyons of the Ancients left their homelands almost two centuries earlier. Some moved to Chaco Canyon or Mesa Verde, while others migrated south to New Mexico and Arizona and are the ancestors of the modern Zunis and Hopis. Canyon of the Ancients is bordered by canyons on its northern and eastern boundaries, and it surrounds Hovenweep National Monument on its western boundary at the Colorado/Utah border.

If Durango is the gateway to Mesa Verde, then the neighboring towns of Dolores and Cortez are the archaeology epicenter for the Four Corners and the entire Southwest. Cortez is just twenty miles west of Mesa Verde National Park and Dolores is ten miles north of Cortez.

Dolores is the home of the Anasazi Heritage Center, a museum that interprets hunter-gatherer and Ancestral Pueblo cultures. There are two twelfth-century archaeological sites on the grounds, named after the Spanish priest explorers, Escalante and Dominguez. Some of the three million artifacts discovered in the area are on permanent display at the museum, and it is also the visitor center for Canyons of the Ancients National Park, about ten miles west of Cortez.

Also within fifty miles of Cortez are Hovenweep National Monument, the Ute Mountain Tribal Park, Crow Canyon Archaeological Center, Yucca House National Monument, and Canyons of the Ancients National Monument. And Cortez is the closest town to the Four Corners National Monument just thirty-four miles way.

Ancestral Puebloan tower at Canyons of the Ancients National Monument near Cortez, Colorado. LEFT: A Lakota Sioux dances the Grass Dance at the Cortez Cultural Center, an example of pan-tribal powwow participants. TOP: Lowry Pueblo, Canyons of the Ancients National Monument, Colorado.

HOVENWEEP NATIONAL MONUMENT

In the Paiute and Ute language, Hovenweep means "deserted valley" because of all the ancient empty dwellings built along sixteen miles (twenty-six km) of Cajon Mesa. The people of Hovenweep built one-story towers around 1000 CE, and began three-story pueblos by 1160 CE. After a twenty-three-year drought starting in the late 1200s, the Hovenweep people left their pueblos. At that time, all over the Four Corners region, smaller communities left as well. The majority migrated to live with the Hopi people in Arizona and the Pueblo people on the Rio Grande River in New Mexico.

 5. The Southeast Quadrant

AZTEC, NEW MEXICO

Aztec, New Mexico, is one of the few places where you can leave your motel room, drive less than two miles across town, and visit a well-preserved prehistoric ruin. The Ancestral Puebloans built beside the Animas River, and so did the Anglo pioneers who founded the town in 1887. But just like Montezuma Castle in Arizona was misnamed after an Aztec leader, these New Mexico founders chose the same faraway Mexican culture. Aztec is thirty-seven miles south of Durango and thirteen miles south of the Colorado/New Mexico border. Like Durango, one of Aztec's most important roles is as an entryway to the many prehistoric ruins in the area.

AZTEC RUINS NATIONAL MONUMENT

Since Chaco Canyon is fifty miles south of Aztec, and Mesa Verde is thirty-five miles north in a fairly straight line and each is situated on the banks of a river, this community was likely a stopping place for traders.

Ancestral Pueblo habitation is indicated from 1050–1300 CE, the end of the Pueblo II and part of the Pueblo III (also known as the Great Pueblo) period. The site includes residential, public, ceremonial, and storage buildings, some three stories high with T-shaped doorways.

The Great Kiva at Aztec Ruins National Monument was rebuilt in the 1930s with funds from the Carnegie Institution and U.S. government's Works Progress Administration. TOP: The masonry at Hovenweep National Monument comes in a magnificent assortment of shapes, including D-shaped buildings and circular and square towers.

The showpiece of the ruins is the Great Kiva, one of the largest and best restored in the Southwest. Great kivas are much larger and deeper than those found at Chaco Canyon and other sites. Their walls come up above ground where the others are completely underground, and they always stand alone, as the central room of a great house. The great kivas have a continuous bench around their inner walls, and are most likely the Mesa Verde region's first public buildings. The Great Kiva at Aztec Ruins was reconstructed in 1934, funded in part by the Public Works Administration, one of President Franklin D. Roosevelt's New Deal programs. The kiva at Aztec Ruins was recreated so visitors can better experience this seven-hundred-year-old space. Putting this in perspective, Notre Dame Cathedral was being completed in Paris at this time.

SALMON RUINS

Eleven miles south of Aztec Ruins, Salmon Ruins near Bloomfield, New Mexico, is another river community, but this one is on the San Juan River. Around 1090 CE a group of Ancestral Puebloans migrated north from Chaco Canyon forty-five miles to this site. The great house was three stories high, had a tower, and contained more than 280 rooms. The inhabitants abandoned the area after a fire destroyed most of the buildings in the 1280s. The ruins are on the south side of Highway 64 in Bloomfield, New Mexico. A mile farther west, the Salmon Ruins Museum displays the best artifacts found at the site, including textile samples and rock art.

FARMINGTON, NEW MEXICO

Ancestral Puebloans lived in the Farmington area, followed by Utes, Jicarilla Apaches, and Navajos several centuries later. The Navajos called the place Tóta´—where three rivers meet.

Spanish explorers followed the rivers to this spot and settled thirty miles east of it in the early 1800s. The western half of San Juan County (Farmington is situated in about the center) became part of the Navajo Nation after the Treaty of 1868, and the government opened the eastern half of the county to settlement in 1872. The non-Indian population began to grow in the 1870s. First the town was called Junction City and then it changed to Farmingtown, later shortened to Farmington. By 1901 the town was surrounded by a thriving farm and ranch community.

Mining companies began investing in oil and gas exploration in the 1920s, but production was low until the 1950s. Farmington's population increased when the San Juan Basin Natural Gas Pipeline was constructed in 1953.

In 1967 the U.S. government joined with the El Paso Natural Gas Company to conduct Project Gasbuggy, an early fracking experiment about fifty miles east of Farmington. They lowered a 29-kiloton surplus atomic bomb into a natural gas well and detonated it, fracturing a huge volume of underground bedrock, thus making more natural gas.

Farming, ranching, and tourism are major economic factors now, and there are probably more high-quality Indian trading posts per square block in Farmington than anywhere else in the Southwest, except Taos and Gallup.

SHIPROCK: THE TOWN

Other than the *straight* lines where the states come together, just about all the other lines within 150 miles of the quadripoint are arcs, serpentines, circles, or that ancient spiritual favorite, the spiral. So far, this book has tried to conform to a spiral as much as possible.

Twenty-six miles west of Farmington along the San Juan River, Shiprock (Naat'aani Nez —"tall leader or tall boss" in Navajo) sits at its own quadripoint where east-west Highway 64 intersects with north-south Highway 491. Bureau of Indian Affairs superintendent William Shelton, called "Tall Boss" by the Navajos, began an irrigation program here in 1903 using San Juan River waters.

Helium, natural gas, and oil were discovered close to Shiprock in 1921, and subsequent exploration and mining helped make the Navajos one of the nation's richest tribes. Uranium was discovered in 1918 in the Carrizo Mountains 135 miles away in Arizona. About 21,300 tons of ore containing about one million pounds of vanadium was shipped from the Carrizo mines between 1942 and 1945 and about 76,000 pounds of uranium was used for the creation of the world's first atomic bombs. However, all known ore bodies in the Carrizos were depleted by 1966. In 2016, Shiprock's population was 8,295 with 96 percent of those people listed as Native American. The Northern Navajo Fair is held there every October and the town has hosted the Shiprock Marathon and Relay footraces since 1984.

In addition to the older traditions of weaving and silversmithing, the relatively new Navajo folk art, which includes clay sculpture, woodcarving, and beadwork, has expanded creative and commercial avenues for Navajo artists. Until 1961, when Navajo medicine man Charlie Willeto began to carve wooden figurines, it was believed that inaccurate or damaged carvings brought bad luck to the artist and the person or spirit it represented. Today more and more artists are teaching themselves to carve and sculpt in this new blend of traditional and contemporary art. The works are usually made from cottonwood, ranging from four inches to five feet tall, and painted with acrylics, watercolors, or even housepaint. Subjects range from traditional spiritual characters, everyday life on the reservation, to whimsical polka-dotted chickens. Some of the best examples of this art form can be found in trading posts in Shiprock, Farmington, and Teec No Pos.

SHIPROCK: THE ROCK

Ten miles southwest of the town of Shiprock and rising 1,583 feet (482.5 m) above the surrounding plain, looms the volcanic plug known as Shiprock, called the Winged Rock by the Navajos. It also fits the geological definition of a monadnock or inselberg—an isolated knob, ridge, rock hill, or small mountain that rises abruptly from a flat plain or gentle slope. It plays an important part in Navajo spiritual traditions. Like Church Rock and Agathla Peak, this mass of lava was level with the plain when the magma rose up to ground level but did not erupt and form a volcano. As the surrounding swamps and seas receded, the Colorado Plateau turned to desert and eroded, leaving Shiprock standing alone. The Navajos say that Monster Slayer and He Who Cuts Life Out of the Enemy vanquished a man-eating eagle here. The sharp pinnacles on top are feathers pointing to the sky.

NAVAJO LAND, NAVAJO WATER

The Treaty of 1868 that allowed the Navajo people to return to their homeland from the Bosque Redondo also provided for farmland and agricultural assistance, but no action was taken to put the stipulations into practice. Four decades later in 1908 the United States Supreme Court then ruled on an Indian reservation water rights case, *Winters v. United States*. The Court then created the Winters Doctrine to define American Indian water rights. This case set a precedent for all Indian reservation water rights and continues to do so today.

After almost a century since the Treaty of 1868, the United States Congress passed Public Law 87-483 in 1962 to provide water for farmland in New Mexico's San Juan River basin. It called for the preparation of 110,630 acres and the diversion of 508,000 acre-feet from the Navajo Reservoir. Finally, in 1972, when the irrigation systems were built and ready to deliver water to the land, the Navajo Nation Council developed the Navajo Agricultural Products Industry (NAPI) to create employment for tribal members and to operate a profitable agribusiness. With 72,000 acres of fields in production, NAPI is now one of the largest contiguous farmland areas in the United States and ships its products all over the world. Alfalfa, corn, barley, oats, potatoes, and beans are their high-quality crops grown under the Navajo Pride brand.

NAVAJO MINING

In addition to farming and raising livestock, mining plays a large part in the Navajo Nation's economy. The Four Corners contains huge reserves of coal, natural gas, oil, and uranium. It's estimated that two major American coal companies, Peabody, and Pittsburgh and Midway, extract more than 23 tons of coal per year there. In 1991 oil wells produced 6.1 million

barrels and 4.5 million cubic feet of natural gas production. Along with uranium, these products have been a major factor in the Navajo economy for almost a century.

CROWNPOINT, NEW MEXICO

Eighty-three miles south of Farmington you'll find Crownpoint, a town of 2,630 people on the Navajo Reservation, founded as an Indian Agency in 1912. It has a high school, a health-care facility, Navajo Technical University, a branch of Diné College, a grocery store, a convenience store, and a gas station.

But it also has Crownpoint Elementary School, which has made Crownpoint famous with rug collectors from all over the world, because of their Navajo rug auction. Hundreds of the finest hand-woven rugs are sold from fifty to thousands of dollars. The weavers themselves display and sell their rugs, and the sale of just one rug can sometimes help sustain a family for a year. The auction is almost always on the second Friday of the month. Viewing starts around 4:30 and the auction starts at 7:00. It's always best to check first by visiting www.crownpointrugauction.com or calling (505) 786-5302 or (505) 786-7386.

TRAIL OF THE ANCIENTS— NEW MEXICO BRANCH

In New Mexico, a second network of roads leading to archaeological and geological landmarks is included under the same name as the group of Utah roads mentioned previously. In New Mexico however, the list of landmarks includes contemporary Native American cultural sites.

Starting at the end and working backward, Farmington is at the northernmost part of the trail. From there we go southwest almost into Arizona to the Toadlena Post Office and Two Grey Hills Trading Post, then down Highway 491 along the Arizona/

Wild horses still thrive on the Navajo Reservation. OPPOSITE: Twenty-eight miles west of Farmington, New Mexico, and just 25 miles southeast of the Four Corners monument, the volcanic plug named Shiprock towers 1,583 feet (482 meters) above the Colorado Plateau.

New Mexico border to Gallup, south again to the Zuni Pueblo near where Conquistador Francisco Vázquez de Coronado first battled with Native Americans in 1540. The trail goes east from there to El Morro Rock, then Grants, New Mexico, for the New Mexico Mining Museum and south to the El Malpais National Monument. From there the trail goes north to Casamero Pueblo, a Chacoan outlier, then Crownpoint, and finally to the starting point of the spiral-shaped trail at Chaco Canyon, a major ceremonial center.

CHACO CULTURE
NATIONAL HISTORICAL PARK

Chaco Canyon lies atop the vast Colorado Plateau, surrounded by the San Juan, San Pedro, and Chuska Mountains and is considered the most important archaeological site in North America. The area contains more than 4,000 prehistoric and historic sites spanning more than 10,000 years of human habitation in Chaco Canyon. Seventy campsites dating from 7000 to 1500 BCE relate to the Archaic Early Basketmakers. Pit houses are found in the canyon that date to 490 CE in the Late Basketmaker II Era, and then around 800 CE the Pueblo I Era culture built crescent-shaped stone complexes with four or five

Chaco Canyon pueblos are noted for their T-shaped doorways. OPPOSITE: San Jose de la Laguna Mission Church, Laguna Pueblo, New Mexico, is twenty-five miles west of Albuquerque on Old Route 66.

rooms next to underground kivas.

Chaco Canyon was home to the Ancestral Puebloans from 850 to 1150 CE, and eventually housed more than a thousand residents known for outstanding achievements in astronomy, agriculture, and architecture. Chacoans hauled more than a quarter of a million trees over long distances and quarried sandstone blocks to construct fifteen large complexes whose buildings were the largest in North America until the early 1800s. The centerpiece of this ancient city is Pueblo Bonito, the largest of sixteen great houses. Shaped like a capital letter "D," the building contained at least 650 rooms and was constructed over three centuries from 850 to 1150 CE.

Although Chaco culture began in this canyon, the culture's influence spread beyond the San Juan River Basin. Chaco culture impacted an area of roughly fifty miles east to west and 150 miles from north to south connected by a network of roads, often with stone curbs, that served as trade routes to outlying areas. The destinations included Canyon de Chelly, Mesa Verde, Aztec Ruins, and Salmon Ruins. These sites are known for their "great house" and "great kiva" architecture style that began, and was perfected, in Chaco Canyon. Trade goods ranged from copper bells and tropical birds from Mexico to turquoise and other precious stones from all over the Southwest.

As with Mesa Verde National Park, UNESCO also declared Chaco Culture National Historical Park a World Heritage Site in 1987 for its archaeological significance. And in 2013, it became an International Dark Sky Park as well.

LAGUNA PUEBLO

"Into the night the overland passenger train,
Slabs of sandstone red sink to the sunset red,
Blankets of night cover 'em up. Night rain gods,
night luck gods, are looking on."

—CARL SANDBURG, *Slabs of the Sunburnt West*, 1922

Laguna means "small lake" or "lagoon" in Spanish, and the one on the Laguna tribal reservation used to be the only lake in New Mexico. Long ago the native people created the lake by building a dam there, but is has now transitioned to meadowlands. The word *pueblo* becomes confusing here because it is the Spanish word for "town" or "village" but the native people themselves were called Pueblos because they lived in so many villages along the Rio Grande near Albuquerque. So, in this area you will find a lot of Pueblo pueblos. To make things easier, the tribal group is spelled with a capital letter while a lowercase one denotes a village, or in this case a group of villages. The Lagunas call themselves KaWaikah or Ka-waik, meaning "lake people." They lived in the transitional area between the Ancestral Pueblo people to the north and the Mogollon culture to the south. The archaeological evidence indicates habitation

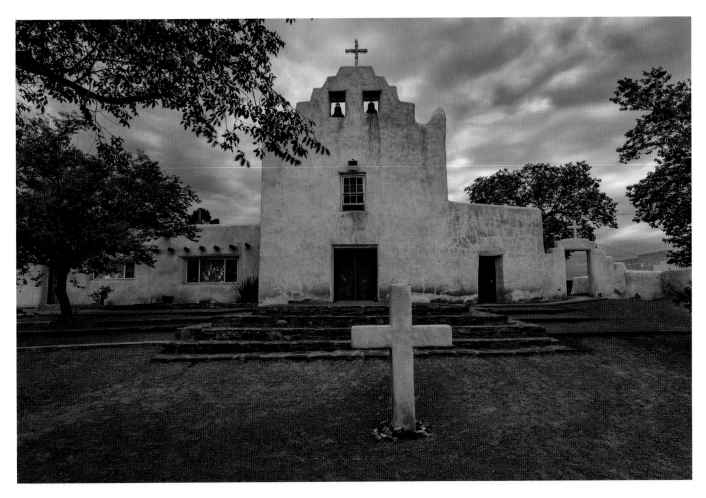

as early as 3000 BCE, but these Lagunas have been there since 1300 CE.

After the Pueblo Revolt and the Spanish returned twelve years later, many people who lived near Albuquerque moved forty-five miles west and established Laguna Pueblo. It is the largest of the Keresan-speaking locations and includes six small villages: Encinal, Laguna, Mesita, Paguate, Paraje, and Seama. There are more than 7,000 registered Laguna tribal members, the largest group of Keresan-speaking tribes. They built outward from the main village into the soft yellow sandstone slopes along the San Juan River.

Each village has a church, but St. Joseph Church in Old Laguna is the most prestigious. The San Jose Mission was constructed in 1699 in Laguna Pueblo and is built of adobe, fieldstone, mortar, and plaster, unlike others of that era. The church interior is 22 feet wide and 105 feet long, with just one door and one small window underneath the twin bells over the door.

In 1880 the Atlantic and Pacific Railroad was working its way westward from Albuquerque on its way to Southern California, and the Laguna Pueblo leaders allowed them to lay track through their reservation if the railroad employed tribal members, which set a precedent used by other tribes as well.

Livestock was the economic base until uranium was discovered in 1951. Mining companies leased 7,868 acres from 1953 until 1982 when the price of uranium dropped and mines closed. The tribe then revived their pottery making and other crafts, built a casino resort, and started a construction company. The tribe also has five semiprofessional baseball teams. Another thing that makes Laguna Pueblo stand out is that Route 66 runs right through it.

THE FOUR CORNERS MEETS ROUTE 66

In 1912 the Texas, Oklahoma, and Kansas Good Roads Associations formed the Mid-Continental Highway Association, and fourteen years later the famous "Mother Road" was born. The legendary Route 66 highway started in Chicago, crossed the heart of the Southwest, and eventually reached its destination on the shores of the Pacific Ocean in Santa Monica, California, 2,448 miles away. Plans became official in 1926 and the road was completed by 1938.

Business boomed in America in the 1920s, especially for Henry Ford, who perfected the Model T automobile, the first car a working man could afford. Even better, you could buy on the installment plan; drive now and pay later. Then companies began offering paid vacations, but most important, Hollywood was hitting its stride, and in addition to the silver screen, it reached middle-class America through a bevy of movie magazines and the newest entertainment source, the radio. Thousands came down with Hollywood fever and had to go see the stars in person, or at least their footprints in front of Grauman's Chinese Theatre.

Route 66 became their magical yellow brick road, taking the fastest diagonal route from the Midwest to Hollywood. Once again, geography favored the Colorado Plateau; its ancient ocean beds offered a flat route south of the Rocky Mountains.

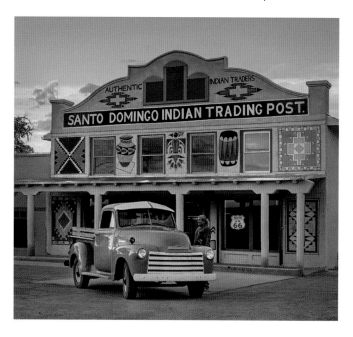

The legend grew for the same reason other American legends did: publicity and marketing. Like the Harvey Company and Santa Fe Railway that preceded it, Route 66 became a major distribution network for Native American arts and crafts. According to Margaret Moore Booker in *Southwest Art Defined: An Illustrated Guide*, quite a few trading posts on Route 66 stopped carrying high-quality native-made goods and just sold cheap mass-produced items. However, several towns along Route 66 through the Four Corners, like Gallup, Holbrook, and Winslow, continue to sell fine native-made art sold in quality trading posts and galleries.

Route 66 enters New Mexico from Oklahoma and roughly follows the 35th parallel north and the Santa Fe Railway route horizontally across the Colorado Plateau, passing through Albuquerque, Laguna Pueblo, Grants, and Gallup, and maintains a straight line along what is now Interstate 40 through Holbrook, Winslow, and Flagstaff.

Route 66 was replaced by interstate freeways by 1985, but the song and syndicated TV series *Route 66*, turned this transcontinental highway into an American icon.

THE ÁCOMA AND THEIR SKY CITY

High atop a steep-walled 367-foot sandstone mesa, Ácoma Pueblo rests almost as it did in 1150 CE when it was built, and may be the oldest continuously inhabited community in the United States. The Ácoma people are a federally recognized tribe related to the Keres and connected with Hopi and Zia pueblos.

Ácoma elders say that their name is known as Akome, Acu, Acuo, or Ako and it means "place that always was." Ácomas were probably part of the Mesa Verde migrations of the middle thirteenth century. In addition to Old Ácoma on top of the mesa, there was Casa Blanca, now a Laguna village, and other villages as far as sixty miles away.

The pueblo covers 431,644 acres, and there are 250 dwellings and more than 4,800 members of the tribe. In 1629, Friar Juan Ramirez directed construction of the massive-walled San Estevan del Rey Mission Church on top of the mesa.

In his book *Ácoma: Pueblo in the Sky*, Ward Alan Minge wrote that one of the oldest stories the people of Ácoma tell is about their ancestors coming from a place underground called Shipapu. The first to come from there were sisters, Nautsiti and Iatiku. Everything else came alive when they arrived at Ácoma.

This image of roof ladders at Acoma Pueblo looks like a painting by one of the Taos Society of Artists, who presented new images of the Southwest's ancient beauty to the eyes of the modern world.

TOP: Begun in 1926 and completed in 1938, Route 66 paved the way for the booming automobile tourism business, including the Santo Domingo trading post at Kewa Pueblo (formerly known as Santo Domingo).

FRED HARVEY: HIS COMPANY AND HIS GIRLS

Before all the artists and writers and moviemakers, a young English immigrant created iconic images of the Southwest so strong and crisp that even today these romantic motifs live on in millions of people's imaginations. He made the Grand Canyon, the Hopi Mesas, and the New Mexico Pueblos popular attractions and changed the worldview of the American West from a harsh wasteland to an idyllic wonderland of panoramic views and spiritual people living at one with nature. In less than twenty years, Fred Harvey transformed the American West from a country to be survived and gotten *through* to a "Land of Enchantment" to be traveled *to* and enjoyed.

Fredrick Henry Harvey emigrated from Liverpool, England, in 1853, and after moving up the ladder from potscrubber to busboy to waiter to line cook in no time, he moved to New Orleans and then to St. Louis and by age twenty-one he was a successful restaurateur.

After losing everything in the Civil War, Fred went to work for the Chicago, Baltimore & Quincy Railroad and worked his way up from baggage clerk to freight agent. In 1875 he opened two cafes along the Kansas Pacific Railway but they closed that same year. However, Harvey knew that trackside service was terrible and that the food was barely edible. The Atchison, Topeka & Santa Fe Railway gave him a contract to give it a try, and the first hotel and eating house opened in Florence, Kansas, in 1878. The plan was so successful that in

less than twenty years there were more than a dozen hotels and cafes along the track from Kansas to California.

Fred formed his own Harvey Company but it was so intertwined with the Santa Fe that it was hard to tell which was which. Through a massive image-building publicity campaign using every print media from books to calendars and even matchbooks, the two companies promoted the virtues of the "Indian Southwest" as a perfect vacation destination. Harvey added gift shops in the hotel or next to the depots where excellent Indian craftsmen demonstrated their skills and you could buy the artwork they created. He created the "Indian Department" in the early 1900s that commissioned artists and photographers to convey the beauty of the Native American Southwest.

He also created the Harvey Girls, a Southwestern phenomenon that opened the doors to economic freedom, independence, and adventure for America's single women. The story goes that after a team of waiters got into a drunken brawl in Raton, New Mexico, and couldn't work the next day, Harvey fired them all and replaced them with young women. It probably didn't happen quite that fast, but according to Jesse Rhodes' article, "How the West Was Won . . . by Waitresses" on Smithsonian.com, Harvey began placing ads calling for "intelligent girls of strong character between the ages of 18 and 30."

The usual uniform was a long black dress with its hem no higher than eight inches above the floor, black opaque stockings, black shoes, and white starched apron. They worked twelve-hour shifts, seven days a week. The Harvey Girls were required to live in dormitories with matrons to enforce a 10:30 p.m. curfew. Their contracts also stipulated that they could not get married for one year or forfeit a portion of their base pay. Some say this was the most broken promise in the West.

Everyone knew the Harvey Girls in the 1880s, but by the 1930s their fame faded, as tourists turned their attention to roadhouses and diners on Route 66. But when the MGM musical *The Harvey Girls* came out in 1947 and Judy Garland sang the Oscar-winning song "The Atchison, Topeka, and the Santa Fe" from a railroad car's back platform, moviegoers fell in love with the independent "can-do" Harvey Girls for decades to come. The Harvey family sold the company to Amfac Parks & Resorts in 1968, which was renamed Xanterra Parks & Resorts in 2002.

The new tourism trends offered new opportunities for economic independence for the intrepid Harvey Girls. TOP: Western tourism expanded dramatically as innovative entrepreneur Fred Harvey made the journey more palatable.

Atchison, Topeka, and Santa Fe Railway Company/Wikimedia

Photo courtesy of the Old Trails Museum/Winslow Historical Society

They both took husbands and multiplied, but then Nautsiti went away to the east. Iatiku stayed and gave all the girl children a clan name. The Sun Clan is the oldest and it is named in memory of Nautsiti because she said she was from that clan.

According to Minge, the Ácomas were ambiguous about receiving the Spaniards as friends. Some believed that they were one with all peoples, and that the Spaniards had come from the people of the first Ácoma sister, Nautsiti. Others thought the Spaniards meant to harm them.

Fray Marcos de Niza visited Cibola, near present Zuni Pueblo, New Mexico, in 1539 and said that beyond there were three kingdoms called Marata, Acus, and Tonteac. Acus probably referred to Ácoma. People there wore turquoise hanging from their ears and noses.

In 1573, Antonio de Espejo went north from Zuni with nine men, looking for a lake filled with gold. He visited the Hopis and came back with 4,000 blankets. The Spaniards were friendly at first, and then on the third expedition they burned the Ácomas' fields and homes.

Late in December of 1598 an Ácoma leader named Zutacapan learned that the Spaniards were going to conquer his people. They thought of defending themselves, but had heard of Spanish atrocities and thought the invaders were immortal, so they tried suing for peace. Juan de Oñate sent his nephew, Captain Juan de Zaldívar to meet with Zutacapan. Captain Zaldívar took sixteen men to the top of the mesa on December 4 and demanded food. When the Ácomas refused the order, the soldiers attacked some Ácoma women. After a short conflict, Juan de Zaldívar and eleven of his men were dead.

Governor Oñate was outraged and sent Juan's brother Vicente and seventy men to punish the Ácomas. The battle began on January 22, 1599, and on the third day Vicente took twelve men and a cannon to the top of the mesa.

Five hundred Ácoma were killed and Oñate ordered that each Ácoma male older than twenty-five have his right foot cut off and be enslaved for twenty years. Twenty-four men lost their feet. Males aged twelve to twenty-five were sentenced to twenty years. Sixty of the youngest women were found not guilty and sent to convents near Mexico City, but may have been sold into slavery there. Two Hopi men at the battle each had a hand cut off.

When King Philip III of Spain heard about the atrocity, Juan de Oñate was tried and convicted for cruelty to both natives and colonists. He was banished from New Mexico, but appeals reversed his sentence and the king appointed him head of mining inspectors in Spain, where he died in 1626 at age 76. Some Ácomas escaped their Spanish captors and had rebuilt their pueblo by 1601.

Like their Hopi relations two hundred miles to the west, Ácoma potters are famous for prehistoric pottery styles with thin white walls and black or reddish-brown markings. In addition to flowers, animals, and abstract creatures inspired by the prehistoric Mimbres culture, Ácoma potters include stylized parrots, brought to the pueblos in ancient times by traders from Mexico. They revered the parrots because the Ácoma believed that the birds could talk with the gods.

EL MALPAIS NATIONAL MONUMENT

Malpais means "badlands" in Spanish. The land within El Malpais National Monument was so bad that Spanish maps warned to avoid it. The monument lies between Ácoma and the Arizona/New Mexico border and is one of the most significant volcanic areas in the United States.

There are forty miles of hardened pahoehoe and a'a lava flows, and more than a dozen cinder cones, lava tubes, and ice caves. "Pahoehoe" is Hawaiian for smooth, unbroken basalt lava with smooth, ropy undulating formations. A'a is also basaltic, but it has a rough, rubbly surface and comes in blocks called clinkers. Hiking on the a'a along the Lava Falls Trail feels like you are treading on top of gigantic burnt brownies.

The Candelaria Ice Cave, also known as the Zuni Ice Cave, is one of the most interesting phenomena in all the Four Corners. Situated at 7,851 feet (2,393 m) in a pine and fir forest, it is part of a collapsed lava tube at the base of Bandera Crater east of the Zuni Mountains. Some of the ice may be three thousand years old, and its blue-green glisten comes from reflected sunlight illuminating arctic algae. The cave is closed to the public from November 1 to March 1.

EL MORRO NATIONAL MONUMENT

Forty-three miles southwest of Grants, New Mexico, on the Zuni Mountains' slopes, there are more than a thousand signatures that have been carved into a sandstone wall over more than three centuries. Travelers stopped at a catch basin at the base of some large golden sandstone cliffs here and carved their names on the big flat wall near the pool.

In April of 1605 thirty Spanish soldiers camped among the pines and junipers next to the water, returning from an expedition that took them from the Santa Fe area to the Sea of Cortez below Yuma, Arizona, eight hundred miles away. The Spanish governor of New Mexico probably had one of his men carve the phrase that started the oldest Euro-American graffiti wall in the United States. The soldier carved these words: "Paso Por Aqui el adelantado Don Juan de Oñate del descubrimiento de la Mar del Sur a 16 de April de 1605." Translated as, "Passed by here the conquistador Don Juan de Oñate from the discovery of the sea of the south the 16th of April of 1605."

La Ventana Arch, El Malpais National Conservation Area, adjoining El Malpais National Monument, near Grants, New Mexico.

From October 15th to December 28th,1866, Captain Richard Henry Orton led his Union Army 1st California Column troops from El Paso, Texas, to San Francisco, California. His route took him past El Morro, where he carved this signature. BELOW: The first Navajo Code Talkers were recruited at Fort Wingate, New Mexico. Their language and courage were crucial to winning the war in the Pacific during World War II. OPPOSITE: Allenroy Paquin, artist and musician of Jicarilla Apache and Zuni descent, performing at the Gathering of the Nations Powwow in Albuquerque, New Mexico.

For the next two and a half centuries, El Morro became a favorite stopover on the old Zuni Trail. The cliff is now known as Inscription Rock. When the railroad crossed western New Mexico in 1881 it bypassed El Morro and the signatures ceased to appear.

FORT WINGATE

Before the soldiers and traders came from the United States, this location was called Ojo del Oso (Bear Spring) and it was a popular Navajo grazing spot. Navajos say the place got its name because a bear once lived near there, and a Navajo threw offerings into the water and when his prayers were answered he named the spring after the bear. General Thomas T. Fauntleroy named the first fort after himself, but the name was changed to Fort Lyons when Fauntleroy joined the Confederate Army in 1862. The fort was renamed in honor of U.S. Army Captain Benjamin Wingate, a Union soldier who died on June 1, 1862, from wounds he received in the Civil War Battle of Valverde, New Mexico.

Starting in 1873, Fort Wingate troops took part in the Apache conflicts and recruited Navajo scouts to assist them. In the twentieth century, the fort was an ammunition depot and in 1944 supplied one hundred tons of explosives for the Manhattan Project's first atomic bomb test. But Fort Wingate's most notable role relates to the Indian boarding school founded there in 1925. That's where the first Navajo Code Talkers were recruited in World War II.

CODE TALKERS

The Four Corners is full of interesting people, but none are more heroic than the Navajo Code Talkers, all of whom ded-

icated their lives to freedom. They were not the first Native Americans utilized by the U.S. Army but they were the largest group and developed their own code.

The original concept for the code was suggested by Mr. Philip Johnston, a Los Angeles civil engineer who learned Navajo when his parents were missionaries on the Navajo reservation. Johnston had read about a unit in Louisiana using Native Americans for messaging and realized that the Navajo language would be perfect for the task. Johnston contacted Lt. Colonel James E. Jones, Area Signal Officer, Pacific Fleet, and a demonstration on February 28, 1942, got the whole thing started.

Officials approved a pilot program for thirty Navajos, and U.S. Marine Corps officers began recruiting at the Fort Wingate Indian boarding school in May. The first 29 Navajo recruits created a substitution code using Navajo words corresponding with English that start with letters of the English alphabet. Then the radiomen would speak a chain of non-related words that spelled out the word they wanted to convey. For example, if you take the first letters of the English translations for the Navajo words Moasi (**C**at), Ne-ahs-jah (**O**wl), Be (**D**eer), and Dzeh (**E**lk), that spells CODE.

To further complicate the code, two or three substitute words were used randomly to disrupt the normal pattern of frequency for often-used letters such as "r," "e," "a," "s," and "t," as in "ax," "ant," and "apple" for the letter "a." Then they assigned common Navajo words for more than two hundred military terms not found in their language. A hand grenade was a potato, a tank was a turtle, and bombs were eggs. There was a four-week course with lots of memorizing, and not all passed. The final code was unbreakable and could be transmitted quickly in battle.

National Archives

Navajo graduates were organized as the 382nd Platoon, U.S. Marine Corps. Eventually, more than 432 Navajos were involved in the code talker program during the war. In her book, *Code Talker Stories*, Arizona State University Professor Laura Tohe, daughter of a Code Talker, said that the Navajo men, some as young as fifteen, joined for three main reasons. There was great poverty on the reservation and they could help their families. Also, they believed that the land was their mother and they needed to protect the Navajo Nation and the United States. And in several oral histories, the former Code Talkers also told Laura that they were impressed with the Marine Corps recruiters' dress uniforms, complete with sabers. Some said that it didn't pass their attention that the girls at the boarding school admired them as well.

The Code Talkers served in just about every battle in the Pacific. Major Howard Conner, 5th Marine Division, said, "Were it not for the Navajos, the Marines never would have taken Iwo Jima." Laura Tohe said that she and other relatives didn't know about the Code Talkers' achievements, sometimes until as late as the 1980s. The program was top secret, but also Navajo spiritual tradition teaches that you do not tell stories of violence and war to children.

Information about the Code Talkers was not declassified until 1968, and the men were nationally recognized in 1969 when they each received a special medallion. In 1971 President Richard M. Nixon awarded them a special certificate for "patriotism, resourcefulness, and courage." In 2001 the first twenty-nine Code Talkers received gold Congressional Medals of Honor and the rest of the 432 received silver ones.

Several Navajos suffered spiritual anguish and mental distress, now known as Post Traumatic Stress Disorder. The Blessingway ceremony helped many return to civilian life. They came home with a great respect for education, shared it with their communities, and passed it on to their children and grandchildren.

GALLUP, NEW MEXICO

Neither an ancient city nor a Spanish colony, Gallup began as an American stage stop. After the Civil War, a route known as the Emigrant Trail followed the trail blazed by the Sitgreaves and Beale expeditions along the 35th Parallel North. The Emigrant Trail connected the Santa Fe Trail to Los Angeles, creating a more direct transcontinental route than the previous Butterfield Overland Mail Route.

This new route across the 35th Parallel would become the railroad route, then Route 66, and eventually Interstate 40. But in the 1870s, the only thing near the stage stop was the Blue Goose Saloon, serving travelers, coal miners, and other local citizens. Then in 1881 railroad paymaster David Gallup opened an office near the saloon and in no time the railroad tent city boasted two dance halls and twenty-two saloons.

Then in 1889 the railroad moved their division offices to Gallup and the town grew again, incorporating as a city in 1891. Railroad steam engines burned coal in those days, and there were dozens of coal mines in the Gallup area.

Tourism was a big part of Gallup's economy because of the railroad. The Fred Harvey Company opened the grandiose El Navajo Hotel in 1923, designed by Mary Elizabeth Jane Colter. The front of the hotel faced the railroad tracks and business boomed for two decades, but after World War II more people drove cars instead of taking the train, and El Navajo was demolished in 1957 to expand Route 66 to four lanes. However, the non-profit Southwest Indian Foundation now maintains a museum and information center in the remodeled railroad depot, renamed the Gallup Cultural Center.

Like Monument Valley on the west edge of the Four Corners, moviemakers found Gallup in the 1930s and made several films there. They were the reason for Gallup's most interesting landmark, the El Rancho Hotel. Nicknamed "The World's Largest Ranch House," it was designed by Ron Griffith, brother of the movie mogul, D. W. Griffith. Stars who stayed there included Humphrey Bogart, Kirk Douglas, Errol Flynn, Rita Hayworth, Katharine Hepburn, Burt Lancaster, and that political upstart, Ronald Reagan. El Rancho fell into disrepair but was restored in 1988 by trader Armand Ortega.

One of the largest cities in the Four Corners area with a 2010 Census population of 21,676, Gallup has been called "The Indian Capitol of the World" and also the "Indian Jewelry Capitol" because of its substantial Hopi, Navajo, Zuni, and Acoma population and the Native American health care and government agency offices there, as well as its large number of trading posts, several with historic significance.

Many private enterprises are listed in the back of this book, but Earl's Family Restaurant deserves extra attention because of its unusual tradition. Founded in 1947, Native Americans bring their handcrafted jewelry, pottery, and other items right to your table. As an extra bonus, the restaurant is also on Historic Route 66.

Keeping traditions alive, there are Indian dances on the County Courthouse Plaza at 7 p.m. every night from Memorial Day to Labor Day. In addition, an arts and crafts exhibition and sale called the Gallup Ceremonial is held every August. It features two downtown parades, a ceremonial dance, and a rodeo.

FORT DEFIANCE

In 1851, U.S. Army Colonel Edwin Sumner built the first fort seven miles north of present-day Window Rock in what would become Arizona Territory twelve years later. The fort was abandoned at the start of the Civil War but reopened as Fort Canby in 1863.

The fort was abandoned again and then burned by Navajos in 1864. It was rebuilt as an Indian agency, and became the first licensed trading post after the Navajo Treaty of 1868 allowed the Navajos' return. The first government school on the reservation was established there in 1870. The town of Fort Defiance had a population of 3,624 in 2010, and is surrounded by several outdoor sport and recreation areas.

SILVERSMITHING AND OTHER JEWELRY

While Gallup is the center of Native American jewelry sales in the Four Corners and is a world leader—along with Santa Fe, Oklahoma City, and Scottsdale, Arizona—most of the jewelry is created in all parts of the Four Corners region. Archaeologists have found jewelry made of shell, bone, turquoise, and other stones, but the Navajos were the first to work in silver, making jewelry for themselves and emulating the Spanish ornaments on horse bridles and saddles. Tradition has it that Atsidi Sani was the first Navajo to work with silver, a skill he learned from a Mexican craftsmen, Nakai Tsotse, sometime in the 1850s.

Navajo jewelry makers are known for certain objects and designs. Among the most well known are conchas, from the Spanish word for "shell." These are round or oval domed disks usually from two to six inches in diameter and stamped with patterns using steel dies and often adorned with coral and turquoise stones. A dozen or so disks fastened at fixed intervals on a strap of leather create the ever-popular concha (formerly called concho) belt.

Another piece of treasured jewelry is the squash blossom necklace. The silver squash blossom-shaped pendants represent one of the most prevalent ancient food groups known as the "Three Sisters," corn, beans, and squash. The necklaces appeared on the market by the 1880s and became a popular trade item. Today, traditional formal wear for Navajo women is a flowing patterned skirt, a brightly colored velvet or velveteen blouse, a squash blossom necklace, and often many bracelets and rings.

Many tribes have their specialty arts, and for the Zunis it is fetishes, miniature animals and abstract figures carved from semiprecious or even precious stones, shells, antlers, coral, bone, and other materials. The fetishes were originally used as personal spiritual totems to absorb the characteristics represented by the animals they portrayed. They are usually small,

and are often carried in a pouch with a bundle of other materials tied to them. When used in this way, the fetishes must be blessed by a medicine man. The ones sold as decorative pieces are more accurately called carvings.

By the 1930s the fetishes became realistic sculptures fashioned with hand tools; now electric drills and rotary tools give the artists a hand. Their work dates to their Ancestral Pueblo forebears who used wooden drills, chipped stones, cactus spines, wood, and stone to work the stones and fiber cords to string their beads.

In 1854 U.S. Army survey leader Captain Lorenzo Sitgreaves described a Zuni forge made of adobe and an animal skin bellows. These tools, one an oven that could sustain superhot temperatures and the other a means of blowing air on the fire to make it even hotter, were used to melt silver and pour it into sandstone molds, thus creating pieces of solid silver cast jewelry. The Zunis also cut stones to fit in silver channels, forming inlay work and creating a beautiful mosaic rivaling ancient Egyptian inlay work.

The Hopis are known for their inlay work as well, but are better known for their overlay designs, a process that began in the late 1930s. In this process, two layers of flat silver are shaped the same, and then the artist cuts designs into what will be the top layer with a delicate jewelry saw. The matching bottom layer is then textured or etched and then oxidized with a mixture called liver of sulfur and it turns black. The two layers are then matched and soldered together, creating a shadow effect where the black background piece is visible through the cut-out top piece.

TOP RIGHT: These bracelets by Hopi artist Weaver Selina are perfect examples of the Hopi overlay style. FAR LEFT: Indian jewelry on display at the Turquoise Museum in Albuquerque, New Mexico. ABOVE: Zuni pendant at the Anasazi Heritage Center in Dolores, Colorado.

6. The Tail of the Spiral: Back in Arizona

WINDOW ROCK

Apropos of the famous Four Corners landscape, the Navajo Nation's capital is named after a red sandstone arch, which are often called windows. The Navajos call this location Tségháhoodzání, which means "the rock-with-hole-through-it" or "perforated rock" and the arch has spiritual significance to them. Window Rock is the tribal government headquarters and the home of several U.S. government agencies.

There are several attractions worth visiting in Window Rock, including the Navajo Nation Museum, Navajo Nation Zoo and Botanical Park, and the Memorial Park. Established in 1961, the first Navajo Tribal Museum then moved to the Navajo Arts and Crafts Enterprise back room in 1982, and finally the magnificent seven-million-dollar Navajo Nation Museum and Library opened in 1997. Its extensive archaeological, ethnographic, and art holdings include more than 40,000 photographs, documents, recordings, films, and videos. The focus is on Navajo artists, including weavers, along with historical and cultural exhibits.

Just four hundred feet northeast of the museum's front entrance you will find another treat, the Navajo Nation Zoo and Botanical Park. Founded in 1963 when it housed bears, coyotes, snakes, elk, and even a golden eagle, the park now

offers a much wider variety of animals, birds, fishes, insects, and plants native to the Four Corners area, including Mexican gray wolves, cougars, bighorn sheep, lynx, and Rio Grande wild turkeys.

Window Rock is also the home of Tony Hillerman's fictional detective, Lieutenant Joe Leaphorn, and the host city for the Professional Rodeo Cowboys' Association Rodeo, the Navajo Nation Fair, and the Navajo Nation Treaty Day celebration.

WINDOW ROCK NAVAJO TRIBAL PARK AND VETERANS MEMORIAL

The Window Rock Navajo Tribal Park and Veterans Memorial sits amid tribal government offices. The centerpiece of the park is a bronze statue of a Code Talker kneeling with his field radio placed with an excellent view of the sandstone window in the background. The memorial, built by Navajo people, honors all Navajos who served in the United States armed services. The design came from a combination of Native Vietnam War veterans, Navajo Code Talkers, and Navajo medicine men.

The park forms a traditional medicine wheel surrounded by a circular path and incorporates many symbolic elements, including the four cardinal directions, the four sacred colors, the circle of life, and an eternal fire in the center. There are sixteen tall, angled, steel pillars that represent bayonets and there is also a sanctuary for solitude, healing, and reflection.

The sandstone window rock arch that gave the town of Window Rock its name.

ABOVE: The Navajo Code Talker Memorial was designed and executed by famed Navajo/Ute sculptor Oreland Joe. The memorial was made possible through the Navajo Code Talkers Memorial Foundation, Inc., and was dedicated in 2004.

ANNIE DODGE WAUNEKA

On December 6, 1963, Navajo Annie Dodge Wauneka was one of thirty authors, diplomats, educators, musicians, and a former U.S. Supreme Court justice awarded the first Presidential Medal of Freedom, created by President John F. Kennedy that year. President Lyndon Johnson read, "First woman elected to the Navajo Tribal Council; by her long crusade for improved health programs, she has helped dramatically to lessen the menace of disease among her people and to improve their way of life."

Annie Dodge was born in Deer Springs, Arizona, in 1910. At age eight she survived a mild attack of Spanish Influenza, saw many Navajos die of the disease, and helped the overworked nurse at the Fort Defiance school care for those struck by the pandemic. She was called on again when trachoma became widespread at her school. Later she said, "From my childhood I have been aware of the problems of my tribe and have wanted to help make our people aware of them."

Her father was Henry Chee Dodge, a prestigious Navajo Nation leader, rancher, trading post owner, and chairman of the Navajo Tribal Council from 1941 until his death in 1947 at age ninety. Wauneka left school in the eleventh grade to help her father and political mentor with his duties as head of the Tribal Council. She often accompanied her father on his visits to needy families, reinforcing her awareness of the Navajo Nation's dire need for modern health care.

In 1951, Wauneka became the first woman to be elected to the Council, defeating two other candidates, one of whom was her husband, George L. Wauneka. They met at an Indian boarding school at Fort Defiance and were married in a traditional Navajo ceremony in 1929. He was a rancher like her father, and they lived near Sawmill for a few years and then moved to Tanner Springs, both in northwestern Arizona. The couple had eight children, two of whom died at an early age.

In her decades-long leadership career, Wauneka traveled to villages and clinics all over the Navajo Reservation as a champion of public health, and urged people to move to modern dwellings and improve the reservation's water quality. Frustrated by the objections of tribal medicine makers, she convinced numerous tribal members to adopt a mixture of modern medicine and traditional ways. And she led the way in wiping out tuberculosis among the Navajos in the 1950s.

Wikimedia

Wauneka served as chairwoman of the health committee on the Navajo Tribal Council for almost three decades. She first went to Washington, D.C., with representatives of an advisory council in 1952, and over the years became a vocal presence before the Bureau of Indian Affairs, always wearing traditional Navajo dress and jewelry.

She attended the University of Arizona in the mid-1950s and earned a Bachelor of Science degree in public health. She received an honorary doctorate in public health from the University of Arizona in 1976, and an honorary Doctor of Laws degree in 1996.

Wauneka served on the advisory boards of the U.S. Surgeon General and the U.S. Public Health Service. *Ladies' Home Journal* declared her Woman of the Year in 1976, and the Navajo Tribal Council named her "Our Legendary Mother" in 1984.

Annie Dodge Wauneka continued to advise the Navajo Tribal Council into her eighties and died in November 1997 in Klagetoh, Arizona, at age 87. Navajo Tribal President Albert Hale, another of Annie Dodge Wauneka's grandsons, said, "She made us proud to be Navajo."

ABOVE RIGHT: Annie Dodge Wauneka (1910–1977), nationally known Navajo health-care advocate and first woman elected to the Navajo Nation Tribal Council. ABOVE LEFT: Henry Chee Dodge (1860-1947), Navajo Nation leader.

ST. MICHAEL'S MISSION

On the west edge of Window Rock, St. Michael's is a Franciscan mission founded in 1896 by funds from Reverend Mother Katharine Drexel, founder of the Sisters of the Blessed Sacrament for Indians and Colored People. She was declared a saint in 2000 by Pope John Paul II. While serving at St. Michael's, Father Berard Haile helped create a written version of the Navajo language and compiled one of the first Navajo-English dictionaries. The Navajos called the land *tso hootso* (yellow meadow) and the Spaniards followed suit, calling it Cienega Amarilla (yellow marsh) because of the plentiful wild sunflowers growing there.

Unlike previous Catholics under Spanish and Mexican rule, the priests here learned the Navajo language and incorporated native ceremonies and traditions into their services. They also helped negotiate with lawmakers in Washington to add land to their reservation to accommodate their growing population. By writing thousands of letters and making annual visits to the Capitol, more than 1.4 million acres (5,687 sq km) to the south and east of the original reservation boundary made in 1868 were added to the Navajo Nation. There is also a town of St. Michaels with its own post office and zip code just west of the mission on Arizona Highway 264.

Like something out of a Greek myth, a forest of wood turned to stone and lies exactly where it fell two hundred million years ago. OPPOSITE: Arizona's petrified wood has a wider color spectrum than other locations around the world. The plateau's vibrant sunsets complete the picture.

PETRIFIED FOREST NATIONAL PARK

"Of all the Southwestern Wonderland—the most concentrated area on earth of the earth's greatest natural marvels—the Petrified Forest is the most puzzling."

—CHARLES F. LUMMIS,
West Coast Magazine, January 1912

Petrified Forest National Park's 230 square miles (600 sq km) of semidesert steppes topography, as well as highly eroded and colorful badlands, lie to the north and south sides of Interstate 40 between the Arizona/New Mexico border and Holbrook. The area was declared a national monument in 1906 and a national park in 1962. The Painted Desert overlaps the northern part of the park and is a protected wilderness area.

Fossils in the park include ferns, cycads, ginkgoes, giant reptiles called phytosaurs, several kinds of large amphibians, and early dinosaurs, but as the name suggests, the park is known primarily for its abundance of Late Triassic–period fossils from 225 million years ago, especially the fallen trees.

During the Late Triassic, giant coniferous trees, some taller than modern redwoods, fell into the rivers and were buried by volcanic ash-laden sediments. Groundwater dissolved the ash, leaving silica that then entered the tree cells, where it replaced the organic matter and formed quartz crystals. Like the red in Four Corners sandstone, various mixtures of iron oxide combined with the silica to duplicate almost every tint of the rainbow, including yellow, pink, purple, and green agatized rock. There are probably more colors found in Arizona's petrified wood than any other similar location in the world.

There are three visitor center museums in the combined Petrified Forest/Painted Desert area. At the north entrance off Interstate 40, the Painted Desert Visitor Center has a bookstore, a twenty-minute documentary shown continuously, brochures, hands-on exhibits, a restaurant, gift shop, and even a gas station. Two miles north of the north entrance, the Painted Desert Inn has a family dining room, museum and gallery space, and panoramic desert views. At the south entrance to Petrified Forest National Park off Highway 180 southwest of Holbrook, you will find an impressive visitor center and museum with life-sized prehistoric animal skeleton displays, a bookstore, a gift shop, and several trails that take you up close to the giant petrified logs.

PAINTED DESERT INN

Located about two miles north of Interstate 40 at the entrance to Petrified Forest National Park, the Painted Desert Inn sits on a mesa overlooking the Painted Desert. Built in 1920 as a tourist lodge by entrepreneur Herbert David Lore, the National Park Service purchased the property in 1935, probably because of the Great Depression's effect on tourism. They in turn hired renowned architect Lyle Bennett to remodel the building, implementing popular rustic national park building motifs. Young men from the Civilian Conservation Corps did the work. Architect Mary Colter designed the interior and Hopi artist Fred Kabotie painted the interior murals. The building was reopened in 1938 as a hotel. It is now a museum and has been designated a National Historic Landmark.

NEWSPAPER ROCK, ARIZONA

If you take Petrified Forest road south from the Painted Desert Visitor Center, cross over Interstate 40 and travel another five or six miles, you will reach yet another amazing thing about the Petrified Forest—a second location called "Newspaper Rock," so named for the same reason as the one located in Utah. According to the National Park Service website, "the archeological site known as Newspaper Rock is neither a newspaper nor a single rock." Instead, there are more than 650 petroglyphs pecked on a number of rock faces in a very small area. The petroglyphs were pecked into the dark mineral coating called desert varnish to expose the lighter rock beneath between 650 and 2,000 years ago, and that some of the artists may have lived at Puerco Pueblo about a mile to the north. The viewing distance is quite a ways from the rock itself.

THE PAINTED DESERT

It was named El Desierto Pintado during Francisco Vázquez de Coronado's expedition in the early 1540s, and the name stuck, translated into English as the Painted Desert. Coronado

These petroglyphs at Puerco Pueblo in the Petrified Forest are about a mile and a half north of Newspaper Rock, which may only be viewed from a distance. TOP: These popular eroded mineral mounds in the Painted Desert are aptly named "The Teepees."

was referring to an area east of Petrified Forest National Park but its current application covers much, much more. The Painted Desert runs roughly from thirty miles north of Cameron, almost to the east edge of the Grand Canyon, southeast past Holbrook, and then overlaps the Petrified Forest just short of the Arizona/New Mexico border, covering more than half the width of Arizona.

The Painted Desert badlands are a wonderland of colors from red, white, lavender, gray, orange, pink, and even blue. Over millions and millions of years, nature's elements created this geological parfait. Here fine-grained layers of relatively soft Triassic Chinle Formation mudstone, shale, and siltstone contain the iron and manganese compounds that provide some of the pigments for this desert palette. Thin layers of the more resistant lacustrine limestone and volcanic flows top the mesas and keep the softer rocks from eroding away. Soil erosion, wind, and water continue to erase and repaint the landscape by shifting the sediment and exposing other layers underneath.

HOLBROOK, ARIZONA

When it started out, this town had a name that would please any Western movie director. It was called Horsehead Crossing, a place where you could cross the Little Colorado River with little danger of sinking in quicksand. But like Gallup, Winslow, Williams, and Kingman, this town was eventually named after a railroad man, the Atlantic & Pacific Railroad's chief engineer, Henry R. Holbrook. When the rails reached the crossing in 1866, Holbrook became a railroad boomtown. There have been gold, silver, and oil boomtowns all over the world, and the American West has had more than its share. Boomtowns are often lawless, and Holbrook had a reputation of being one of the wildest towns in the West, as you might guess from its famous Bucket of Blood Street, named after a particularly gory cowboy bar fight.

The town got a little more civilized when Fred Harvey opened one of his first Harvey House trackside cafes in 1884. It was actually a number of bright red railroad cars decorated with Indian-style designs. Route 66 came right through Holbrook and several blocks of it are still there, so fans can eat at Joe and Aggie's Route 66 Café with a mural of the whole road painted on the side of the building, and stay at the Wigwam Motel, where the individual units are shaped like teepees.

HOMOLOVI STATE PARK

Three miles east of Winslow, look for Interstate 40 exit 257 and go north on Highway 87. The Hopi call it Homol'ovi, (pronounced Ho-MOL-oh-vee), and between 600 and 1250 CE small groups of prehistoric people lived in pit houses in the area. Then Hopi ancestors, the Hisat'sinom (ancient ones), farmed the fertile soil near the Little Colorado River and built six pueblos between 1260 and 1290 CE, adding another that archaeologists call Homol'ovi II around 1350 CE. Several decades later, about a thousand people lived in 1,200 rooms with forty kivas arranged around three plazas. According to park officials, visitors are not allowed to take any of the pottery shards left on the ground there. The Hopi believe these will lead Bahana (elder brother) to the site to bring another golden age. Visitors have placed some of the more striking samples along the tops of partially reconstructed walls as a display.

This aerial photo of the Little Painted Desert gives marvelous perspective on nature's sculptural beauty.

LITTLE PAINTED DESERT COUNTY PARK

Drive just north of Homolovi about fourteen miles on Highway 87 and you'll be there. It's just a small pullout park, but it has great views of the Painted Desert. The best time to view something like this is in the late afternoon or early morning when warm, golden light slants to enhance the colors and geological details, and the shadows provide more contrast.

WINSLOW, ARIZONA: MORE THAN JUST A CORNER

Yes, there is a popular song lyric "Standin' on the Corner in Winslow, Arizona" from the 1972 Eagles hit "Take It Easy." And yes, Winslow is the fictional town called "Radiator Springs" in the 2006 Pixar/Disney animated movie *Cars.* But the town also has an important place in United States history and in the hearts of generations of families who lived there.

Like Holbrook, Winslow was also a safe place to cross the Little Colorado River, but it had a more idyllic name then, Sunset Crossing. The Atlantic & Pacific Railroad crews stored their iron rails there so the Navajos called Winslow "iron laying down." Also like Holbrook, the name was changed to honor a railroad man, General Edward F. Winslow.

Winslow is a great old-fashioned walking-around-downtown kind of place with several attractions all within a few blocks. Standin' on the Corner Park includes a statue of a guitar player, a huge mural depicting images from the famous song, and even a red flatbed Ford parked at the curb. Across the street from the park is the Old Trails Museum, whose exhibits portray Winslow's connections with the ancient cultures, the U.S. Army camel expedition, Mormon settlers, trading posts, the Santa Fe Railway, Harvey Girls, and Route 66.

Second Street runs east-west through downtown and was the route of the 1857 Beale Camel Expedition. The railroad runs parallel to it and pulls up right in front of the hotel.

What makes Winslow stand apart from the other railroad towns, however, was, and still is, the La Posada Hotel and train depot. The name is Spanish for "the resting place" and architect Mary Elizabeth Jane Colter designed the hotel, modeling it after the grand hacienda style of the Spanish-Mexican Southwest.

Colter said it was her masterpiece. Opened in 1930, it featured rustic furniture from around the globe, Spanish engravings, wrought-iron fixtures, terra-cotta roof tiles, and Mexican red Saltillo tiles on the floors. But this grand hotel opened in 1930 just after the Wall Street stock market crash triggered the Great Depression. That, along with construction of Route 66 and the auto camping craze, sealed La Posada's fate from the start. But not exactly. The Santa Fe Railway saved it from destruction and made it their division headquarters, maintaining the building until they moved out in 1993. Then architect and artist Allan Affeldt and his artist wife and business partner Tina Mion worked with federal, state, and city support to restore the hotel, which reopened in 1997.

All of the Four Corners is fascinating tourist country, but it was always difficult to reach some of the most interesting locations. So someone at the Fred Harvey Company, perhaps Fred himself, came up with an idea. In 1925 the company created "Indian Detours," specialized auto tours that took passengers off the Santa Fe train for a few days and then returned them to catch a later train to continue their journey.

At first the tours centered around Harvey House hotels in Santa Fe or at the Grand Canyon, but after La Posada was complete in 1930, it became headquarters for tours to the Hopi Mesas, the Petrified Forest, Canyon de Chelly, and Rainbow Bridge.

The fleet of "Harveycars" included Cadillacs, Franklins, Packards, and White Motor Company buses. The drivers were men in stylized cowboy outfits who had at least four years' mechanic experience. And Harvey replayed his Harvey Girls idea by hiring intelligent, attractive young women as tour guides called Couriers. They dressed in Navajo-style uniforms, including velveteen blouses, concha belts, and floppy-brimmed cloche hats with the Harvey Company thunderbird insignia.

The Great Depression and World War II gas rationing put an end to the Indian Detours, and it was replaced by individual automobile tourism after the war.

ABOVE: "Harvey Cars" were oversized touring cars and coaches constructed by Chicago's Yellow Cab Company.

THE LITTLE COLORADO RIVER

Although the vast Colorado Plateau that surrounds the quadripoint where four states meet is mostly an arid or semiarid desert, water always plays its part in the story. Both Holbrook and Winslow are located where they are because of the Little Colorado River.

The Little Colorado is not as dramatic as its bigger namesake, but it has its impressive moments. The biggest one is called the Grand Falls of the Little Colorado. Just east of Flagstaff, when the snow melts and sometimes during the heavy rains and flooding in late summer, the Little Colorado forms a waterfall that drops 185 feet (56 m). This is much more impressive when you consider that Niagara Falls drops only 167 feet (51 m). However, the Grand Falls is not one steep drop like Niagara but rather a series of drops. And very few people have even seen the Grand Falls because they only flow a few weeks out of every year.

Just south of Interstate 40 between Winslow and Flagstaff, Meteor Crater is about 3,900 feet (1,200 meters) in diameter and 600 feet (170 meters) deep. Fifty thousand years ago a nickel-iron meteorite about 160 feet (50 meters) wide struck the earth at eight miles per second (12.8 kilometers per second). The meteorite disintegrated almost entirely with the ten megaton impact. TOP: The magnificent Grand Falls of the Little Colorado near Flagstaff is not well known because it only flows a few weeks a year.

tional traveler, mathematician, and astronomer. In 1894, Lowell hired astronomer A. E. Douglass to find a perfect spot for a new observatory. A hill on the edge of Flagstaff turned out to be just right. The dwarf planet Pluto was discovered from there in 1930, and in the 1960s, the observatory's Clark Telescope mapped the moon for the Apollo lunar expeditions.

Northern Arizona Normal School, a teachers' college, was established in Flagstaff in 1899 and renamed Northern Arizona University in 1966. Their sports teams are known as the Lumberjacks, not what comes to mind for most people when you say "Arizona," but appropriate for their timber industry history. There are several fascinating sites, both archaeological and geological, not far from Flagstaff.

WALNUT CANYON NATIONAL MONUMENT

Nine miles east of Flagstaff just off Interstate 40 is a limestone canyon that formed sixty million years ago. The canyon contains more than three hundred prehistoric Sinagua culture cliff dwellings. Archaeologist Harold S. Colton named the Sinagua for the Spanish phrase for the nearby San Francisco Peaks, Sierra Sin Agua (mountains without water). The Sinagua lived in the canyon from 400–1400 CE and foraged for plants and nuts, including Arizona black walnuts. President Woodrow Wilson created Walnut Canyon National Monument in 1914 in response to local citizens' alarm at the scores of "pot-hunters" armed with dynamite and shovels who destroyed ancient buildings and desecrated graves.

FLAGSTAFF, ARIZONA

Following our spiral route around the Four Corners, we complete the east-west leg along the south edge of the Colorado Plateau in Flagstaff, at the southwest corner of our 150-mile radius from the quadripoint.

With a 2015 population of 70,320, and surrounding areas taking it to 139,097, Flagstaff is the largest city on the edge of the Colorado Plateau and is the favorite jumping-off point for most of the places mentioned in this book and also the Grand Canyon. Flagstaff lies within the largest contiguous ponderosa pine forest in the continental United States, so its early industries were lumber, railroads, and ranching. Eventually, astronomy, education, and tourism were added.

Another distinction Flagstaff has over other cities is its unobstructed view. While the Four Corners is known for its far-reaching views to horizons a hundred miles away, Flagstaff's view is straight up. That view has made it internationally famous, and it all started with Percival Lowell. Lowell came from a wealthy family that settled in Boston in 1639. His family situation gave him the time and funds to become an interna-

From 1100 CE to 1250 CE Ancestral Puebloans built their homes in alcoves along Walnut Canyon's limestone upper ledges.
TOP: Celebrities from Clark Gable to Jon Bon Jovi have stayed at the Hotel Monte Vista in Old Town Flagstaff. The Babbitt Brothers opened their first trading company in 1889 just eight years after the town was founded. OPPOSITE: The San Francisco Peaks are the highest point in Arizona and are just sixty miles from its lowest point at the bottom of the Grand Canyon.

SUNSET CRATER VOLCANO NATIONAL MONUMENT

The Hopis call it Red Hill and the Navajos call it Yellow Top Mountain, but Grand Canyon explorer John Wesley Powell called it Sunset Crater because the reddish-orange cinders at the rim of this dormant volcano made him think of sunset.

Sunset Crater was made by the most recent eruption in the San Francisco volcanic field, an array of six hundred volcanoes covering 1,800 square miles (4,700 sq km) along the Colorado Plateau's southern border. The volcanoes' ages range from six million years old to less than a thousand.

The highest peak in the field is Humphreys Peak, at Flagstaff's northern perimeter. It is Arizona's highest at 12,633 feet (3,851 m) and is part of the San Francisco Peaks, an extinct stratovolcano complex that includes Agassiz Peak, Fremont Peak, Aubineau Peak, Rees Peak, and Doyle Peak, all more than 11,000 feet (3,352 m). Even more astonishing than having this many tall peaks in Arizona is the fact that the bottom of the Grand Canyon, just fifty-four miles away, is at an elevation of 2,200 feet (670 m). The area from the top of Humphreys Peak to the bottom of the Grand Canyon spans five of the six Life Zones described by C. H. Merriam in 1889 from Arctic-Alpine to Upper Sonoran Desert (Lower Sonoran Desert is the only one not represented). The zones fit the area perfectly because Merriam did part of his research on the San Francisco Peaks.

WUPATKI NATIONAL MONUMENT

Isolated and serene on the edge of an arid sagebrush prairie with views to the horizon, the architectural elegance of Wupatki Ruin commands the landscape. Wupatki means "tall house" in the Hopi language. Their traditions say that when their ancestors came up from an earlier world, the holy ones told them to go as far in all four directions as they could to establish their territory.

Sunset Crater in the foreground is backed up by the San Francisco Peaks, which were once part of a giant stratovolcano that may have been four thousand feet taller than the current peaks. OPPOSITE: Day's end at Sunset Crater.

Wupatki's fine masonry rivals that of Mesa Verde or Chaco Canyon. Here, ancient civilization meets the timeless Milky Way.

Situated on the Sunset Crater scenic-loop road north of Flagstaff, Wupatki is one of the fastest and easiest ruins to reach from a major city. It was the largest and tallest pueblo within hundreds of miles, home to about a hundred people, but thousands more lived within a day's journey from there. Although people had lived there for 10,000 years, the volcanic eruption played a part in their development and growth. Some moved there when their homes were destroyed by ash and lava, and others learned that volcanic cinders held moisture for crops. The agricultural community burgeoned, large pueblos like Wukoki, Citadel, and Lomaki were built short distances from Wupatki, and there are an estimated 2,700 archaeological sites scattered over fifty-five square miles (142 sq km) within the monument.

Turquoise, shell jewelry, copper bells, and parrot bones indicate that a far-reaching trade network brought exotic items to the area. Wupatki was a meeting place for many cultures, but its people moved on about 1250 CE. The Hopis say the place was not abandoned, and although it was no longer occupied, Wupatki is remembered and revered by the descendants of its residents.

CAMERON TRADING POST

As with several other locations in northeastern Arizona, the first non-Indians to live there ran a trading post fifty-two miles north of Flagstaff at what is now the junction of Highways 89 and 64. The latter is the east entrance road to the Grand Canyon. They chose the location because of something to do with water, as usual. This time the water-related item was a treacherous suspension bridge over the Little Colorado River. Hubert and C. D. Richardson built the Little Colorado Trading Post out of sandstone in 1916 so that local Hopis and Navajos could trade their livestock, blankets, and wool for dry goods and hardware. The place was later named Cameron after Ralph Cameron, U.S. senator from Arizona, 1921–1927.

In the 1920s, with better roads and affordable cars, Cameron became a stopping place on the way to the Grand Canyon. The post has been remodeled and is still operating today.

Cameron Trading Post carries a wide variety of Native American art and crafts, like this Acoma pot. TOP: Established in 1916, original proprietors Hubert and C.D. Richardson named the post in honor of Arizona Senator Ralph Cameron.

EPILOGUE

There are many spirals in this book, just as there are in history. There are geological cycles from desert to wetlands, then oceans, and then back to deserts. The patterns repeat themselves for millions of years to create the Colorado Plateau's spectacular formations. Human civilizations cycle too, from clans and bands to villages, towns, and empires, then reverting to villages again, mostly as weather cycles changed over thousands of years.

But a spiral is not a circle, repeating itself over and over again the same way. On the map, we started at the quadripoint and spiraled outward. In the broad universal sense, ancient civilization seems to do this as well. Starting with pit houses and progressing all the way to four-story apartment complexes, then reverting to smaller-scale houses but never going all the way back to living in caves. Modern history is similar, more of a "two steps forward and one step back" situation, except it's not a straight linear progression. Some aspects of life advance while others regress. The beauty of experiencing the depth of the Four Corners' geography, geology, archaeology, and Native American cultures is that we get to see the big, big picture with many different points of view, and ponder our place in such a vast universe.

NATIONAL, STATE, AND TRIBAL PARKS OF THE FOUR CORNERS

ARIZONA

FOUR CORNERS MONUMENT
(928) 206-2540

GLEN CANYON NATIONAL RECREATION AREA
(928) 608-6200

HOMOLOVI STATE PARK
(928) 289-4106

HUBBELL TRADING POST NATIONAL HISTORIC SITE
(928) 755-3475

MONUMENT VALLEY NAVAJO TRIBAL PARK
(435) 727-5870

NAVAJO NATIONAL MONUMENT
(928) 672-2700

PETRIFIED FOREST NATIONAL PARK
(928) 524-6228

SUNSET CRATER VOLCANO NATIONAL MONUMENT
(928) 526-0502

VERMILION CLIFFS NATIONAL MONUMENT
(435) 688-3200

WALNUT CANYON NATIONAL MONUMENT
(928) 526-3367

**WINDOW ROCK NAVAJO TRIBAL PARK
AND VETERANS MEMORIAL**
(928) 871-6647

WUPATKI NATIONAL MONUMENT
(928) 679-2365

COLORADO

CANYONS OF THE ANCIENTS NATIONAL MONUMENT
(970) 882-5600

COLORADO NATIONAL MONUMENT
(970) 858-3617

MCINNIS CANYONS NATIONAL CONSERVATION AREA
(970) 244-3000

MESA VERDE NATIONAL PARK
(970) 529-4465

NEW MEXICO

AZTEC RUINS NATIONAL MONUMENT
(505) 334-6174

CHACO CULTURE NATIONAL HISTORICAL PARK
(505) 786-7014

EL MALPAIS NATIONAL MONUMENT
(505) 876-2783

EL MORRO NATIONAL MONUMENT
(505) 783-4226

RED ROCK PARK
(505) 722-3839

UTAH

ANASAZI STATE PARK MUSEUM
(435) 335-7308

ARCHES NATIONAL PARK
(435) 719-2299

BEARS EARS NATIONAL MONUMENT
(435) 587-1510

CANYONLANDS NATIONAL PARK
(435) 719-2313

CAPITOL REEF NATIONAL PARK
(435) 425-3791

DEAD HORSE POINT STATE PARK
(435) 259-2614

EDGE OF THE CEDARS STATE PARK MUSEUM
(435) 678-2238

GOOSNECKS STATE PARK
(435) 678-2238

GRAND STAIRCASE-ESCALANTE NATIONAL MONUMENT
(435) 644-1200

HOVENWEEP NATIONAL MONUMENT
(970) 562-4282

NATURAL BRIDGES NATIONAL MONUMENT
(435) 692-1234

NEWSPAPER ROCK STATE HISTORIC MONUMENT
(435) 587-1500

RAINBOW BRIDGE NATIONAL MONUMENT
(928) 608-6200

SHOPPING AND PLACES OF INTEREST

ARIZONA

ARIZONA OFFICE OF TOURISM
(866) 275-5816
www.visitarizona.com

FLAGSTAFF

LOWELL OBSERVATORY
(928) 774-3358

MUSEUM OF NORTHERN ARIZONA
(928) 774-5213
www.musnaz.org

**NORTHERN ARIZONA UNIVERSITY
CLINE LIBRARY**
(928) 523-5551
www.nau.edu/special-collections/
exhibits

**PIONEER MUSEUM
ARIZONA HISTORICAL SOCIETY**
(928) 774-6272
www.arizonahistoricalsociety.org/
museums/welcome-to-pioneer-
museum-flagstaff

CAMERON

CAMERON TRADING POST
(928) 679-2231
www.camerontradingpost.com

NAVAJO ARTS & CRAFTS ENTERPRISES
www.gonavajo.com

NAVAJO TRAIL TRADING POST
(928) 697-3613
www.navajotrailtradingpost.com

PAINTED DESERT TRADING COMPANY
(928) 679-2312
www.painteddeserttrading.com

CHAMBERS

NAVAJO TRAVEL CENTER
(928) 688-2293

HOLBROOK

**NAVAJO COUNTY
HISTORICAL SOCIETY MUSEUM**
(928) 524-6225
http://holbrookazmuseum.org

WIGWAM MOTEL
(928) 524-3048
www.galerie-kokopelli.com/wigwam

HOUCK

CHEE'S INDIAN STORE
Houck, AZ
(928) 688-2433
www.cheesindianstore.com

ORTEGA INDIAN CITY ARTS
Houck, AZ
(928) 688-2691

KAYENTA

CODE TALKER EXHIBIT AT BURGER KING
(928) 697-3534

GIFT SHOP AT THE HAMPTON INN
(928) 697-3170

**GIFT SHOP AT THE
MONUMENT VALLEY KAYENTA INN**
(928) 697-3221

GIFT SHOP AT THE WETHERILL INN
(928) 697-3231

NAVAJO ARTS & CRAFTS ENTERPRISE
(928) 328-8120
www.gonavajo.com

NAVAJO CULTURAL CENTER
(928) 697-3170

KEAMS CANYON

MCGEE'S INDIAN ART
(928) 738-2295
www.hopiart.com

LUPTON

TEEPEE TRADING POST
Lupton, AZ
(928) 688-2596

MONUMENT VALLEY

**GIFT SHOP AT GOULDINGS LODGE AND
CAMPGROUND**
(435) 727-3231
www.gouldings.com

GIFT SHOP AT THE VIEW HOTEL
(435) 727-5555
http://monumentvalleyview.com

PAGE

CARL HAYDEN VISITOR CENTER
(928) 608-6200
www.nps.gov/glca/planyourvisit/
visitorcenters.htm

POWELL MUSEUM
(928) 645-3412
www.powellmuseum.org

SANDERS

INDIAN RUINS INDIAN STORE
(928) 688-2787

R. B. BURNHAM & COMPANY
(928) 688-2777
https://rbburnhamtrading.com

SECOND MESA

HOPI CULTURAL CENTER AND MUSEUM
(928) 734-2401
www.hopiculturalcenter.com

TSAKURSHOVI
(928) 734-2478

TEEC NOS POS

TEEC NOS POS TRADING POST
(928) 656-3224

TUBA CITY

EXPLORE NAVAJO INTERACTIVE MUSEUM
(928) 640-0684

GIFT SHOP AT MOENKOPI LEGACY INN
(928) 283-4500

TUBA CITY TRADING POST
(928) 283-5441

TUUVI TRAVEL PLAZA
(928) 283-4500

WINDOW ROCK

NAVAJO ARTS & CRAFTS ENTERPRISE
(928) 871-4090
www.gonavajo.com

NAVAJO NATION MUSEUM
(928) 871-7941
www.navajonationmuseum.org

**NAVAJO NATION ZOO
AND BOTANICAL PARK**
(928) 871-6574
www.navajozoo.org

ST. MICHAELS MUSEUM
(928) 871-4171
www.discovernavajo.com/
museums.aspx

WINSLOW

LA POSADA HOTEL
(928) 289-4366
http://laposada.org

OLD TRAILS MUSEUM
(928) 289-5861
www.oldtrailsmuseum.org

STANDIN' ON THE CORNER PARK
http://standinonthecorner.com

WINSLOW ARTS TRUST
(928) 587-8934
http://winslowartstrust.org

COLORADO

**COLORADO TRAVEL AND TOURISM
AUTHORITY**
(800) COLORADO

CORTEZ

CORTEZ CULTURAL CENTER
(970) 565-1151
https://cortezculturalcenter.org

**CROW CANYON
ARCHAEOLOGICAL CENTER**
(800) 422-8975 | (970) 565-8975
http://crowcanyon.org

**NOTAH DINEH TRADING COMPANY
& MUSEUM**
(800) 444-2024 | (970) 565-9607
http://notahdineh.com

DURANGO

A SHARED BLANKET
(970) 247-9210
www.asharedblanket.com

**DURANGO & SILVERTON
NARROW GAUGE RAILROAD MUSEUM**
(888) 872-4607

POWERHOUSE SCIENCE CENTER
(970) 259-9234
https://powsci.org

**SOUTHERN UTE CULTURAL CENTER
& MUSEUM**
(970) 563-9583
www.southernute-nsn.gov/
southern-ute-museum

TOH-ATIN GALLERY
(970) 247-8277
www.toh-atin.com

SILVERTON

**MINING HERITAGE MUSEUM
& 1902 COUNTY JAIL**
(970) 387-5609
http://sanjuancountyhistoricalsociety
.org

TELLURIDE

**AH HAA SCHOOL FOR THE
ARTS/HISTORIC TRAIN DEPOT**
(970) 728-3886
www.ahhaa.org

TELLURIDE HISTORICAL MUSEUM
(970) 728-3344
www.telluridemuseum.org

NEW MEXICO

NEW MEXICO TOURISM DEPARTMENT
(505) 827-7400
www.newmexico.org

AZTEC

AZTEC MUSEUM AND PIONEER VILLAGE
(505) 334-9829
www.aztecmuseum.org

AZTEC SANDSTONE ARCHES
(505) 334-7551
www.aztecmuseum.org

FARMINGTON

ALEX BENALLY S HOGAN
(505) 564-3404

ANIMAS RIVER TRAILS-BERG PARK
(505) 599-1400
farmingtonnm.org/listings/
animas-river-trails

ARTIFACTS GALLERY
(505) 627-2907
http://artifacts-gallery.com

FARMINGTON MUSEUM
(505) 599-1174
www.fmtn.org/248/Farmington-
Museum-at-Gateway-Park

FARMINGTON NATURE CENTER
(505) 599-1422
www.fmtn.org/252/Riverside-
Nature-Center

FIFTH GENERATION TRADING COMPANY
(505) 326-3211
www.southwestshowroom.com

SAN JUAN COLLEGE
(505) 326-3311
www.sanjuancollege.edu

SHIPROCK TRADING POST
(505) 324-0881
www.shiprocktradingpost.com

SHIPROCK

FOUTZ TRADING COMPANY
(505) 368-5790
www.foutztrade.com

NAVAJO ART & CRAFTS ENTERPRISE
www.gonavajo.com

GALLUP

BILL MALONE TRADING COMPANY
(505) 863-3401
http://billmalonetrading.com

BUTLER'S OFFICE SUPPLY
& SOUTHWESTERN BOOK NOOK
(505) 722-6661
www.butlersofficecity.com

ELLIS TANNER TRADING COMPANY
(505) 863-4434
www.etanner.com

EL MORRO THEATRE
(505) 726-0050
www.elmorrotheatre.com

EL RANCHO HOTEL
(505) 863-9311
www.route66hotels.org/
attractions-in-new-mexico

FIRST AMERICAN TRADERS
(505) 722-6601
www.firstamericantraders.com

GALLUP MAIN STREET ARTS
AND CULTURAL DISTRICT
(505) 399-2890
www.gallupculturaldistrict.org

NAVAJO TRAVEL PLAZA
(505) 863-3118

NIGHTLY INDIAN DANCES
(505) 722-2228
http://nightlyindiandances.com

ORTEGA'S INDIAN ARTS & CRAFTS
(505) 863-3919

RICHARDSON'S TRADING
(505) 722-4762

THUNDERBIRD JEWELER'S SUPPLY
(505) 722-4323
www.thunderbirdsupply.com

USA RV PARK
(505) 863-5021
www.usarvpark.com

WILD SPIRIT WOLF SANCTUARY
Ramah, NM
(505) 775-3304
https://wildspiritwolfsanctuary.org

ZUNI PUEBLO
(37 miles south of Gallup)
(505) 782-7238
www.zunitourism.com

UTAH

UTAH OFFICE OF TOURISM
(800) UTAH-FUN

BLANDING

THE DINOSAUR MUSEUM
(435) 678-3454
dinosaur-museum.org

GREEN RIVER

GALLERY MOAB FINE ART
(435) 355-0024
https://gallerymoab.com/works

JOHN WESLEY POWELL
RIVER HISTORY MUSEUM
(435) 355-0024

MOAB

MOAB GIANTS DINOSAUR PARK
(435) 355-0288
http://moabgiants.com

MOAB INFORMATION CENTER
(435) 259-8825
www.discovermoab.com/
visitorcenter.htm

ACKNOWLEDGMENTS

I would like to thank geologist Mark Thoman, author Leo Banks, and the staff of numerous national parks and monuments covered in this book for their detailed and well-researched website information pages. I am also grateful to the Arizona Historical Society, History Colorado, New Mexico Office of the State Historian, and the Utah Historical Society.

— JIM TURNER

A special thanks to my lovely wife, Wendy, who adds so much to my world with original guitar songs, art projects, meals with homegrown vegetables, vases filled with garden flowers, and so much more. It's a joy coming home after days and weeks of travel.

I would like to especially thank Nina Rehfeld for being an enthusiastic adventure buddy, Ron Ayers for sharing his curiosity and musical talents on many road trips, and Bill Niehues for safely piloting several flights for aerial photography. Thanks also to pilots Russell Gerbace in New Mexico, and Ted Grussing in Arizona, for photography time in the air.

Thank you to my fabulous web designer Denise Traver, Julia Latka for consistently publishing my work in Europe, Hopi jeweler Duane Tawahongva for sharing his work and friendship, Juanita Edaakie and the Zuni Olla Dancers for a unique photo shoot, Deborah Westfall for access to the collections at Edge of the Cedars Museum in Utah, David Bowyer for his photographic knowledge of the Four Corners, photographer Gary Ladd for sharing the beauty of Lake Powell, Scott Stulberg and Holly Kehrt for photographing together in amazing locations, Bill and Elaine Belvin for an exceptional photography trip to backcountry sites, and to fellow travelers Tory and Meg Harper for your uplifting friendship.

In addition, a hearty thank you goes to Ray Begay, Gary Tso, Diné medicine woman Walking Thunder, Allenroy Paquin, Norman and Ramona Roach, Laurent Martrés, Kathleen Bryant, Jim Hook, Stephen DeNorscia, Bob Ross, Dawn Aley, Miguel Valdivia, Patrick A. Bailon, Turquoise Museum in Albuquerque, and Scott Thybony.

— LARRY LINDAHL

ABOUT THE AUTHOR

JIM TURNER earned his master's degree in U.S. history from the University of Arizona in 1999 and has been researching and teaching Arizona history for more than forty years. Jim retired as Arizona Historical Society historian in 2009 to write *Arizona: A Celebration of the Grand Canyon State* and is currently an author and editor for Rio Nuevo Publishers where he wrote *The Mighty Colorado River: From the Glaciers to the Gulf* and *Crater Lake and Beyond: The Land of Fire and Ice.* Jim also gives history presentations for Roads Scholars (formerly Elderhostel), is a presenter for the Arizona Humanities, and gives presentations at conferences, conventions, and retirement communities in Tucson and Phoenix.

ABOUT THE PHOTOGRAPHER

LARRY LINDAHL is a travel and nature photographer with a passion for the colorful Southwest. He explores the region frequently to photograph its diverse cultures, sculptured geology, and awe-inspiring vistas. His landscape photography has been exhibited by the Smithsonian Institution and is permanently displayed at Petrified Forest National Park. He has five photography books to his credit, several with publishing awards, along with images on international magazine covers and in feature stories about the Southwest. His work appears in *Arizona Highways, Outdoor Photographer, Backpacker, Southwest Art,* and *Conde Nasté Traveler.* He is the author of *Secret Sedona: Sacred Moments in the Landscape* and lives in Sedona, Arizona.